Home Bible Study

Commentaries

from

The Gospel

of

John

by

LARRY D. ALEXANDER

REVISED SECOND EDITION

OTHER BOOKS ON CHRISTIANITY BY LARRY D. ALEXANDER INCLUDE:

* *Sunday school lessons from the book of the Acts of the Apostles*
* *Sunday school lessons from the Gospel according to John Mark*
* *Sunday school lessons from the Apostle Paul's letter to the Romans*
* *Home Bible study commentaries from the Gospel of John*
* *Home and Church Bible study commentaries from the book of Hebrews*
* *Home and Church Bible study commentaries from Paul's letter to the Romans*

INTRODUCTION

Larry D. Alexander is a well-known visual artist, turned Christian teacher and author, who was called by GOD, more than eleven years ago, to learn and teach HIS Holy Word, without help from the institutions of men. He understood his calling to be that his training in the Word was to be infused in him, through direct guidance from GOD, through the HOLY SPIRIT, and that GOD will always lead him spiritually to the right material, people, and sources that he needs, in order to successfully do HIS Will. Alexander says GOD instructed him to began to write down, and retain in writing, those things that he had learned, and then, to share them with others. Alexander has been teaching Sunday school and bible studies for the past ten years.

This book is written to help revive the interest of adults in building themselves up in the Word of GOD by attending Home and Church Bible studies and Sunday school classes in their respective Christian churches, and, to start up, or restore Bible studies and Sunday school classes back to those Christian churches that are lacking these opportunities to get to know CHRIST JESUS, our LORD. Alexander strongly believes that the only thing that can change a man or woman for the better is the Word of GOD.

All of Alexander's books are designed to promote spiritual growth and right-living in those who choose to read and incorporate GOD's directives into their everyday lives. The teaching commentaries that are presented in this book, as well as Alexander's previous books are bold and straightforward. They are to be used to help introduce people to JESUS through a study of the words and actions that were demonstrated to us by JESUS, during HIS three-year ministry here on earth, and, through the work of the Apostles and others who were instrumental in the development and establishment of the early Christian Church. Again there is a strong focus on developing good Christian living practices and behavior, and, on developing a fear and reverence for the ONLY WISE GOD, WHO is our SAVIOR, through JESUS CHRIST, HIS SON, WHO sent to us, the HOLY SPIRIT.

II

HOW WE GOT OUR BIBLE

Much has been written about how GOD inspired men to write the pages of the bible. GOD used about forty men to write the scriptures and some of these authors remain a mystery even today. The writers of the last chapter of Deuteronomy, the book of Job, and many of the Psalms are classic examples of biblical texts with unknown human authors. We do not have a single manuscript in the handwriting of Moses, Isaiah, Paul, or any other original writer.

That of course always leads to this eternal question, "How do we know that the bible we have today is the written word of those original writers who were inspired by GOD? We already know that GOD did not inspire all those who copied, or translated the bible into various versions, as HE did the original writers. It is quite evident to those who study to be scholars, that, while the original writers were guided and kept from making mistakes by the power of GOD, both copyists and translators were not, and, could and did make errors.

Even though we have no part of the bible in the handwriting of the original writers, we do have two kinds of sources from which we can learn what the original writers wrote. These sources are called "manuscripts" and "versions". "Manuscripts" are documents written by hand. In the days before printing was invented, this was the only way of producing books. There are no known bible manuscripts that were written by the original authors available to man today.

However, we do have many copies of manuscripts that were copied from the original manuscripts, or, copies of them. "Versions" are translations of a document into a different language. Some of our ancient versions were actually translated from copies of manuscripts older than any we have today. Therefore, they help us to know exactly what the original writers wrote.

The Old Testament books were written in the Hebrew and Aramaic languages between 1400 and 400 B.C. The oldest bible "manuscript" copies we have today were the ones found among the now famous "Dead Sea Scrolls" in 1947 and later. These copies date back to circa 100 B.C. The oldest known "version" of the Old Testament is the Greek version known as the "Septuagint", which was written by seventy Jewish scholars in Alexandria, Egypt in about 250 B.C., from Hebrew manuscript copies older than any we have today.

In the first half of the second century the bible was translated into Syriac, and not much later, into Latin. A more careful Latin version was completed, around 400 B.C. by the famous scholar, Jerome, called the "Vulgate", which means "common and proper". This version became the official bible of the Roman Catholic Church, and, of Western Europe. Made from very ancient manuscript copies, this book helps us to be sure the bible we have is approximately the same as the original writings.

In 1380 John Wycliffe and his team of scholars translated the bible into "middle English", a blend of "Norman French and Anglo-Saxon languages. This version was translated directly from the Latin Vulgate. In 1525, William Tyndale wrote an

English version of the New Testament. He later translated some of the Old Testament books into English. His version was translated directly from the original Hebrew and Greek manuscript copies. English churchmen angrily opposed Tyndale's version, and they, along with king Henry VIII, decided instead to go with an English version written by Myles Coverdale. Coverdale used the Latin Vulgate and Martin Luther's German version for his translations.

In Geneva, Switzerland, William Wittington and his group of scholars wrote a revised English version that came to be known as the "Geneva Bible" in 1560. Some of the marginal notes in the Geneva bible offended the Bishops of the Church at England, and this led to the writing of the "Bishops Bible" in 1568. Through the remainder of that century, the Bishop's Bible and the Geneva Bible were split among the churchmen in popularity.

In 1604, however, King James I appointed a commission of 54 scholars, led by Robert Barker, to write a new English version of scriptures. They mostly followed the Bishop's Bible, but they also consulted other English translations, along with the German, Greek and Hebrew text, the Syriac, the Septuagint, and several Latin versions. In 1611 they completed the book that went on to become the most printed and used text in the history of the English Language, "The King James Version" of the Bible.

But as the world would have it, all living languages are constantly changing. Many words used in the King James Version are now unknown, or obsolete. Some examples are "nessing", "besom", and "wist". Other words have actually changed their meanings. For example "let", in those days, meant, "to hinder" (Romans 1:13). Now, however, it means, "to permit". The word "conversation", in those days meant "your whole way of living", but today it just means, "talk".

Today, just like in the old days, every Christian needs a bible, translated in their modern native tongue, and in this country that means a "New Living Translation" version of the bible. No translation, or version has ever been translated without error, and that includes the "King James Version". And the reason that it has never been done is because there has never been a perfect scholar, or perfect man period, except CHRIST JESUS, and HE didn't choose to write one personally.

But most of our available versions are good enough to familiarize us with the word of GOD that has been handed down to us, both orally and written, since the foundation of this world. We should trust that GOD is still with us, just as HE was with the original writers. And while we may think or believe that there may be no more inspired writers, I believe more so that GOD still wants us to get to know HIM through HIS word, and the best way we can understand HIS word is in our own modern-day language.

So let's just try and retire the King James Version to our library of reference books, where it can serve us in our studies most efficiently. GOD wants us to get to know HIM and just like in all generations before us, HE raises up scholars to interpret HIS word into our own present-day languages.

Larry D. Alexander

III

INTRODUCTION TO THE GOSPEL OF JOHN

It is the belief of most scholars that the Gospel of John is the fourth Gospel. It was most likely written sometime between A.D. 85 and 95. John's depiction of JESUS is the most theological of the four Gospel accounts. He presents to us, a JESUS WHO existed with GOD, and, as GOD, even before the creation of the universe itself. John's unique style confronts us with an overwhelming necessity to believe on our LORD and SAVIOR JESUS CHRIST. He presents JESUS as the focus of a cosmic struggle between light and darkness, truth and deceit, love and hate, and most of all, life and death.

When we read the text of this book, the author's name is not given, however this is not unusual, as none of the other gospels identify human authors either. Oftentimes an author may indirectly reveal himself within his writing, and this book of John is no exception. It is also the external evidence that lends ascription of authorship of this text to the Apostle John, because it was a well-known fact to the early church, that the Apostle penned this Gospel account.

The four Gospels are our only primary sources of information about CHRIST JESUS, and while they do not present us with a biography of HIS life, they do present us with a very clear picture of HIS PERSON, HIS works, and, the way HIS FATHER GOD intended for us to live and serve. Even the accounts of HIS ministry are anything but exhaustive, and by John's own admission, much is left unrecorded\ regarding HIS wonderful works (John 21:25). The Gospel of John, like all the other Gospels, gives considerably more coverage to the events of the last week of JESUS' life than it does anything else.

Each Gospel writer seems to deliberately try to emphasize a slightly different aspect of the life of CHRIST and HIS works, but none of the writers seem to observe a strict chronological order. In fact, all four Gospels are much more interpretation, than they are chronicles, with Luke's Gospel coming the nearest to being chronologically in order.

Scripture gives us considerably more information about John than it does about any of the other Apostles. John Mark tells us in his Gospel that John was the brother of James, and son of Zebedee (Mark 1:19). He also tells us that John and James worked with the "hired servants" of their father (Mark 1:20). Most scholars agree that John's mother was Salome, one of the women who observed JESUS' crucifixion (Mark 15:40). And, if Salome were the sister of Mary, JESUS' mother (John 19:25), then, that would make the Apostle John a cousin of JESUS.

John may not have been as outspoken as the Apostle Peter, but he did possess a bold personality that served him well at the time of JESUS' death. We know this, because scripture tells us that he was the only apostle, who dared to stand at the foot of cross, on that terrible day of JESUS' crucifixion at Golgotha.

Jewish tradition tells us that John was obedient to JESUS' command to take care of HIS mother Mary, and he did so, while pasturing a church in the city of Ephesus, the city where Mary is said to have died. Tertullian, the great Church Historian, tells us that the Apostle John, who lived longer than all of the original disciples, was taken into Rome in his later years, and plunged into boiling oil, and was miraculously unhurt. He was then exiled to the Greek island of Patmos, where he later penned the book of Revelation, after receiving his, now famous, vision from JESUS CHRIST.

Jerome, the author of the "Vulgate", the first Latin translation of the bible, tells us in his commentary on Galatians, that, when the Apostle John was old in age and could no longer walk, they used to carry him into the temple. At that time, his sermon consisted of one sentence; "Little children, love one another". It is an astounding testimony to the affirmation and belief that John had in his heart, for the doctrine and teachings of CHRIST JESUS.

He was a man who was truly prepared for spiritual service to the LORD. He had thoroughly learned from the instructions of CHRIST JESUS, and he lived a long life in conformance to the will and ways of the MASTER TEACHER. And perhaps, John, with his own life, demonstrated to us more clearly than all the other disciples that, "JESUS is Faithful", "JESUS is longsuffering", and, most of all, "JESUS is love".

CONTENTS

CONTENTS

CONTENTS

CHAPTER ONE:

JESUS IS GOD IN HUMAN FORM

SCRIPTURE:
The King James Version
(John 1:1-34)

1 (1) In the beginning was the WORD, and the WORD was with GOD, and the WORD was GOD. **(2)** The SAME was in the beginning with GOD. **(3)** All things were made by HIM; and without HIM was not any thing made that was made. **(4)** In HIM was life; and the life was the light of men. **(5)** And the light shineth in darkness; and the darkness comprehended it not. **(6)** There was a man sent from GOD, whose name was John. **(7)** The same came for a witness, to bear witness of the LIGHT, that all men through him might believe. **(8)** He was not that LIGHT, but was sent to bear witness of that LIGHT. **(9)** That was the true LIGHT, which lighteth every man that cometh into the world. **(10)** HE was in the world, and the world was made by HIM, and the world knew HIM not. **(11)** HE came unto HIS own, and HIS own received HIM not. **(12)** But as many as received HIM, to them gave HE the power to become the sons of GOD, even to them that believe on HIS name: **(13)** Which were born, not of blood, nor of the will of the flesh, nor of the will of man, but of GOD. **(14)** And the WORD was made flesh, and dwelt among us, (and we beheld HIS glory, the glory as of the only begotten of the FATHER,) full of grace and truth. **(15)** John bear witness of HIM, and cried, saying, "This was HE of WHOM I spake, HE that cometh after me is preferred before me: for HE was before me. **(16)** And of HIS fullness have all we received, and grace for grace. **(17)** For the law was given by Moses, but grace and truth came by JESUS CHRIST. **(18)** No man has seen GOD at any time; the only begotten SON, which is in the bosom of the FATHER, HE hath declared HIM. **(19)** And this is the record of John, when the Jews sent priests and Levites from Jerusalem to ask him, "Who art thou?" **(20)** And he confessed, and denied not; but confessed, I am not the CHRIST. **(21)** And they asked him, "What then?" "Art thou Elias?" And he saith, "I am not". "Art thou that prophet?" And he answered, "No". **(22)** Then they said unto him, "Who art thou? that we may give an answer to them that sent us. What sayest thou of thyself?" **(23)** He said, "I am the voice of one crying in the wilderness, make straight the way of the LORD, as said the prophet Esaias. **(24)** And they which were sent were of the Pharisees. **(25)** And they asked him, and said unto him, "Why baptizest thou then, if thou be not that CHRIST, nor Elias, neither that prophet?" (26) John answered them, saying, "I baptize with water: but there standeth one among you, whom ye know not; (27) He it is, who coming after me is preferred before me, whose shoe's latchet I am not worthy to unloose. (28) These things were done in Bethabara beyond Jordan, where John was baptizing. (29) The next day John seeth JESUS coming unto him, and saith, "Behold the LAMB of GOD, which taketh away the sin of the world. (30) This is HE of WHOM I said, after me cometh a MAN which is preferred before me: for HE was before me. (31) And I knew HIM not: but that HE should be made manifest to Israel, therefore am I come baptizing with water". (32) And John bare record, saying, "I saw the SPIRIT descending from Heaven like a dove, and it abode upon HIM. (33) And I knew HIM not: but HE that sent me to baptize with water, the SAME said unto me, "Upon WHOM thou shalt see the SPIRIT descending, and remaining on HIM, the SAME is HE which baptizeth with the HOLY GHOST. (34) And I saw and bare record that this is the SON of GOD".

COMMENTARY:

The "King James Version" of John chapter one is perhaps my favorite stretch of passage in all of Scripture to read, if for no other reason than the sheer beauty and flow of the Apostle John's writing as the words are translated to the Old English of the 17th century, as a result of the work done by Robert Barker and the team of 54 scholars who were commissioned by King James.

In verses 1-14, the Apostle John seeks to put the Word of GOD into perspective, and show us the true power of its meaning, and, its effect on the world. Here John reminds us that the Word of GOD is already here, and in fact, has been with us since the beginning of time, and it simply cannot be, nor will not be disregarded. We cannot ignore GOD's Word and get away with it. It has always been, is now, and will forever be synonymous with life. It is effective and penetrating, and it absolutely scrutinizes all of our thoughts, desires, and intentions.

In the biblical Greek, the term used for "word" is "logos" (log-os), and it, more or less, emphasizes the message of that which is spoken. Here John expresses to us that our LORD and SAVIOR, JESUS CHRIST personifies the Word of GOD, in the flesh. He is trying to get us to understand that one of the key reasons for JESUS' first advent, was and is, for "communication". JESUS is the "Spoken Word", and "Living Expression" of all that which GOD ever sought to communicate to us about HIMSELF. John is saying, particularly in verse 1, that, JESUS is both, "identical" to the GOD of the Old Testament concept, and yet, is distinct from HIM.

One can imagine how stunning this must have been to the people of the first century. Even today, many people have a problem with embracing this concept, which has now become familiar, and yet still remains just as mysterious as it ever was. Here though, we can see that, while the concept may be difficult, John's teaching seems to be very clear. He is saying that JESUS existed eternally with GOD the FATHER, as one GOD, yet, with a distinct and separate personality. Those of us, who understand the concept which unity in a family and marriage represents, can certainly grasp the concept of "unity as one" between the FATHER and the SON.

In John chapter 1, verses 6-34, the Apostle John writes of the fulfilling of the role of the "witness" John the Baptist, that had first been prophesied by Isaiah some 700 years earlier (Isaiah 40:3), and then again by the prophet Malachi 300 years later (Malachi 3:1). John the Baptist was born to be the "forerunner" for JESUS' ministry, and he fulfilled his mission well. He came to announce the coming of the "bearer" of the gift of Salvation.

It is true that in human society, if someone hands someone else a gift, and that person doesn't perceive that gift to be real, then they probably aren't going to reach out and accept it. Our believing in GOD, in all of HIS fullness, can be likened to that. GOD is giving us the gift of eternal life through HIS only begotten SON, JESUS the CHRIST. Believing in HIM involves seeing HIM as real, and, as coming from GOD, and then, reaching out and accepting HIM. By accepting JESUS, one also accepts GOD the FATHER's wonderful gift of eternal life in Heaven, and, at one and the same time, becomes what they weren't before, and that is, quite simply, "a child of GOD".

JESUS came into the world to teach us how to live our lives perfectly under GOD, and, to teach us how to die and live again with GOD. HE taught us how to give and forgive, and, HE taught us how to love, and how to give thanks. John points to JESUS as being the LIGHT of the world, a true light for all people. In HIM we see exactly what GOD is like, and only HE can usher us into GOD's OWN glorious presence, without fear, without guilt, and, without shame.

THE FIRST DISCIPLES
(John 1:35-51)

1 (35) Again the next day after John stood, and two of his disciples; (36) And looking upon JESUS as HE walked, he saith, "Behold the LAMB of GOD!" (37)

And the two disciples heard him speak, and they followed JESUS. (38) Then JESUS turned, and saw them following, and saith unto them, "What seek ye?" They saad unto HIM, "Rabbi, (which is to say, being interpreted, MASTER,) where dwellest THOU?" (39) HE saith unto them, "Come and see". They came and saw were HE dwelt, and abode with HIM that day: for it was about the tenth hour. (40) One of the two which heard John speak, and followed HIM, was Andrew, Simon Peter's brother. (41) He first findeth his own brother Simon, and saith unto him, "We have found the MESSIAS", which is, being interpreted, the CHRIST. (42) And he brought him to JESUS. And when JESUS beheld him, HE said, "Thou art Simon the son of Jona: thou shalt be called Cephas", which is by interpretation, a stone. (43) The day following JESUS would go forth into Galilee, and findeth Philip, and saith unto him, "Follow ME". (44) Now Philip was of Bethsaida, the city of Andrew and Peter. (45) Philip findeth Nathanael, and saith unto him, "We have found him, of WHOM Moses in the Law, and the prophets, did write, JESUS of Nazareth, the SON of Joseph". (46) And Nathanael said unto him, "Can there any good thing come out of Nazareth?" Philip said unto him, "Come and see". (47) JESUS saw Nathanael coming to HIM, and saith of him, "Behold an Israelite indeed, in whom is no guile!" (48) Nathanael saith unto HIM, "Whence knowest thou me?" JESUS answered and said unto him, "Before that Philip called thee, when thou wast under the fig tree, I saw thee". (49) Nathanael answered and saith unto HIM, "RABBI, THOU art the SON of GOD; THOU art the KING of Israel". (50) JESUS answered and said unto him, "Because I said unto thee, I saw thee under the fig tree, believest thou? Thou shalt see greater things than these." (51) And HE saith unto him, "Verily, verily, I say unto you, Hereafter ye shall see Heaven open, and the angels of GOD ascending and descending upon the SON of MAN."

COMMENTARY:

The initial contact that JESUS made with men who would later become HIS disciples was made when John the Baptist pointed CHRIST out to two of his own disciples. The two men curiously followed after JESUS, and when the MESSIAH looked around and saw them, HE asked them what it was that they wanted. The two men requested to know where it was that JESUS was staying, and JESUS invited them to come and see.

It was about four o'clock in the afternoon, and they went with JESUS and abided with him for the remainder of the day. One of these men was named Andrew, and he was the brother of Simon Peter. After spending the afternoon with JESUS, the first thing Andrew thought about doing was bringing his brother Peter on board, by giving him the good news about CHRIST. He runs and tells his brother that he has found the long-awaited MESSIAH, and he then takes him back to meet JESUS.

Those three men were the first to get to know JESUS in the literal sense. Today we get to know JESUS through HIS written word, and by associating with HIS people, or those who genuinely believe on HIM. The word, "know", in John 1:31 means to "recognize". John the Baptist knew JESUS spiritually, (He saw the doves descend on JESUS and remain with HIM) and because of that, he recognized JESUS was without sin. That is why John initially refused to Baptize JESUS (Matthew 3:14). It was because John's baptism was for sinners, and he knew JESUS, WHO was without sin, had no reason for repent, and thereby, had no need for his baptism. He probably felt that, to baptize the MESSIAH, at best, would be an insult, and at worse, would be blasphemous.

The next day JESUS decided to go to Galilee, where HE found Philip and invited him to be HIS disciple. Philip was a native of Bethsaida, Andrew and Peter's hometown. Now the first thing Philip does, is, go and find Nathanael, who was an honest man, to tell him the good news about CHRIST. After learning that JESUS was from Nazareth, a curious Nathanael asks, "Can anything good come from there?"

After coming face to face with JESUS, JESUS shows Nathanael a bit of HIS supernatural knowledge by telling him of HIS knowledge of Nathanael's character and reputation of being an honest man. JESUS also discloses to him that HE had already seen him "underneath a fig tree", an expression that often meant "in a place of safety and leisure".

Impressed by JESUS' knowledge of him, Nathanael was prompted to confess JESUS as both the "SON of GOD" and the "KING of Israel". Throughout Scripture, JESUS refers to HIMSELF as the "SON of Man" more than 80 times, and in this particular passage, we are presented with one such occasion. It is a term that speaks of HIS humanity and suffering, and, of HIS work as the ideal man. In other words, HE sought to convey to us that HE had come to be a living, human example of what the life of every man, who wishes to worship GOD in Spirit, and in Truth, should be like.

WHAT DID WE LEARN FROM CHAPTER ONE?
Here are some key points to remember

(1). CHRIST existed in the beginning with GOD, and HE is inseparable from the

FATHER. (John 1:1)

(2). GOD created everything that exists, and HE is, in fact, LIFE ITSELF. HE is LORD over both the physical and spiritual life. (John 1:4-5)

(3). GOD sent John the Baptist to be a witness and forerunner to CHRIST JESUS. (John 1:6-9)

(4). We, are not children of GOD by way of our human existence, but rather, we are children of GOD, only when we believe in, and accept CHRIST as our LORD and SAVIOR. We are then given the right to become children of GOD, by GOD HIMSELF. (John 1:12)

(5). JESUS CHRIST, THE WORD, became flesh, so that HE could dwell among us long enough to show us a living, performing example of how GOD wants us to live lovingly and faithfully, here on earth. HE sought to show us, through HIS words and actions, just what GOD THE FATHER is like. (John 1:14)

(6). We have all benefited from the rich eternal blessings that CHRIST has afforded us with, through HIS vicarious sacrifice on the cross at Golgotha. (John 1:16)

(7). Like these first disciples, when we come to know CHRIST JESUS, we should be eager to go out and tell someone else the "Good News" of the great things HE has done for all mankind in general, and all Christians in particular. (John 1:35-51)

CHAPTER TWO:

THE FIRST SIGN OF THE MESSIAH

SCRIPTURE:
The King James Version
(John 2:1-12)

2 **(1)** And the third day there was a marriage in Cana of Galilee; and the mother of JESUS was there: **(2)** And both JESUS was called, and HIS disciples, to the marriage. **(3)** And when they wanted wine, the mother of JESUS saith unto HIM, "They have no wine". **(4)** JESUS saith unto her, "Woman, what have I to do with thee? MINE hour is not yet come". **(5)** HIS mother saith unto the servants, "Whatsoever HE saith unto you, do it". **(6)** And there were set there six waterpots of stone, after the manner of the purifying of the Jews, containing two or three firkins apiece. **(7)** JESUS saith unto them, "Fill the waterpots with water". And they filled them up to the brim. **(8)** And HE saith unto them, "Draw out now, and bear unto the governor of the feast". And they bare it. **(9)** When the ruler of the feast had tasted the water that was made wine, and knew not whence it was: (but the servants which drew the water knew;) the governor of the feast called the bridegroom, **(10)** And saith unto him, "Every man at the beginning doth set forth good wine; and when men have well drunk, then that which is worse: but thou hast kept the good wine until now". **(11)** This beginning of miracles did JESUS in Cana of Galilee, and manifested forth HIS glory; and HIS disciples believed on HIM. **(12)** After this HE went down to Capernaum, HE, and HIS mother, and HIS brethren, and HIS disciples: and they continued there not many days.

COMMENTARY:

The now famous "wedding at the village of Cana" in Galilee, is regarded as the site of the first of the "seven signs", or "miracles", of the MESSIAH, that are recorded in the Gospel of John. It was a private miracle, known only to Jesus' disciples, a few wedding servants and quests, and Mary, the mother of JESUS.
Of the four Gospel writers, only the Apostle John was present at this wedding. John, perhaps, uses the word "sign", instead of "miracle", so that he might draw away from the spectacle of the event, in order that we may be better able to focus on the significance of the event.

The "turning of the water into wine" is also the first of any of the 35 miracles of JESUS that are recorded in all of the four Gospels combined. It occurred three days after JESUS' calling of Philip and Nathanael. JESUS' disciples, HIS mother, and, HIS brothers were all invited. A wedding feast of this nature would typically last for seven days, and it would begin following the groom's taking of his bride to his home, or, to his father's home, for consummation of the marriage.

After all of the wine had been consumed (v. 3), JESUS' mother, Mary, turned to HIM for help. In verse 4, JESUS' response, and use of the word "woman" to respond to HIS mother, in those days, was a polite term, even though it may not be for us today. The expression "What have I to do with thee", also in verse 4, in the Greek, was a common expression that referred to a difference in relations, or realms. It also can be translated, "How does that concern you and me", which, would seem more likely what JESUS was stating.

According to Jewish custom, the host at a wedding feast always treated the guests with wine, and the guest's name was mentioned when the wine was poured. The statement spoken by JESUS, "MY time has not yet come" (still in verse 4) may simply mean nothing more than, "It is not MY turn to treat".

JESUS did "treat", however, and the water was miraculously turned into the best wine of all. Six large stone water pots were there, which was normally used for regular Jewish ceremonial purposes. Each pot could hold twenty to thirty gallons of water. JESUS instructed the servants to fill the pots with water. After the pots were filled to the brim with water, JESUS told them to dip some out and take it to the master of ceremony. When the master of ceremony tasted the water that had been transformed into wine by JESUS, he called the bridegroom over and said to him, "Usually the host serves the best wine first, then, when everyone is full and doesn't care, he brings out the less expensive wines. But you have kept the best for last".

Some scholars believe that all of this was a clear signal that Mary must now face the fact that her SON JESUS was now committed totally to the will of HIS FATHER GOD, and to the completion of HIS mission here on earth. And although she had given birth to HIM, and raised HIM from a child, she must now submit herself to JESUS as her LORD and SAVIOR, just like all the rest of humanity would have to do, in the process of time. And while she did not completely understand this at the time, she had decided, from that moment on, to trust in HIM completely.

The, significance of this miracle is explained by John, in verse 11 as the initial manifestation of the glory of CHRIST to men here on earth. JESUS' first miracle of transforming water into wine at a joyful event such as this wedding, was a sign of the joy that HE would bring to all mankind, through "a transformation of hearts". HIS ministry would be a "transforming one", and the transformation that HE would bring, would come by way of the HOLY SPIRIT.

THE CLEARING OF THE TEMPLE AT JERUSALEM
(John 2:13-25)

2 (13) And the Jews' Passover was at hand, and JESUS went up to Jerusalem, (14) And found in the temple those that sold oxen and sheep and doves, and the changers of money sitting: (15) And when HE had made a scourge of small cords, HE drove them all out of the temple, and the sheep, and the oxen; and poured out the changers' money, and overthrew the tables; (16) And said unto them that sold doves, "Take these things hence; make not MY FATHER's house an house of merchandise". (17) And HIS disciples remembered that it was written, "The zeal of thine house hath eaten ME up". (18) Then answered the Jews and said unto HIM, "What sign shewest THOU unto us, seeing that THOU doest these things? (19) JESUS answered and said unto them, "Destroy this temple, and in three days I will raise it up". (20) Then said the Jews, "Forty and six years was this temple in building, and wilt thou rear it up in three days?" (21) But HE spake of the temple of HIS body. (22) When therefore HE was risen from the dead, HIS disciples remembered that HE had said this unto them; and they believed the scripture, and the word which JESUS had said. (23) Now when HE was in Jerusalem at the Passover, in the feast day, many believed in HIS name, when they saw the miracles which HE did. (24) But JESUS did not commit HIMSELF unto them, because HE knew all men, (25) And needed not that any should testify of man: for HE knew what was in man.

COMMENTARY:

In verses 13-25, unlike the three Synoptic Gospels Matthew, Mark, and Luke, John's Gospel account of JESUS' cleansing of the temple at Jerusalem comes at the beginning of JESUS' ministry, rather than near the end. This fact, and, the differences in their narrations, leads most scholars to believe that there were probably two temple cleansings performed by JESUS, during HIS three-year ministry, one at the beginning, which caught the people by surprise, and a second in the third and final year, probably during HIS "passion week". This second cleansing probably contributed more heavily to the Jewish leader's plans and desires to kill JESUS.

At the time of the annual Jewish Passover, JESUS went up to Jerusalem, as was HIS custom, and visited the temple, most likely to teach and preach. However, in the "court of the Gentiles", the outermost court of the temple, the Jews had begun a tradition of buying and selling animals used for sacrifices at the temple, during Passover. They rationalized these activities, as providing a convenience for the pilgrims, who had journeyed into Jerusalem from afar, and needed lambs, or doves, or, needed their currency changed over to the local currency so that they could participate in the Passover rituals and celebrations.

Unfortunately, like all of the best-laid plans of men, abuses soon developed, and pilgrims became, more often than not, victims of scams and high prices, by corrupt dealers and merchants. For instance, they had even begun to charge an admission fee, or dues, in order to enter into the temple during Passover.

When JESUS saw all of this corrupt activity, taking place in the House of GOD, HE made HIMSELF a whip from some ropes and chased all of the merchants and moneychangers, and their livestock, out of the temple. HE then walked over to those who sold doves and instructed them to take their birds and leave the temple also, because they were turning the house of GOD into a marketplace that was attracting robbers and thieves.

When the angry Jewish leaders, who were, no doubt, getting their cut from the temple proceeds, asked JESUS, "What right did HE have to clear the temple?", and, to show them a miraculous sign if HIS authority came from the LORD, JESUS responded by telling them to "Destroy this temple, and in three days I will raise it up".

Now it had been 46 years since King Herod the great had started rebuilding on the temple that Zerubbabel and his crew had constructed, following the Israelites 70-year stint in Babylonian captivity. Herod had decided that he would restore the temple back to the glorious state that King Solomon had brought to it, during his prosperous reign. However, the temple that JESUS spoke of was the temple of HIS OWN body, a statement that the spiritual-less Pharisees were incapable of hearing, and actually, so too were HIS disciples, at that time.

The disciples, however, did recall this statement after JESUS' Resurrection, and because of the many miraculous signs and wonders that JESUS performed at the Passover, many other people were also convinced that HE was truly the MESSIAH. However, JESUS didn't trust them, because HE knew what people were like. After all, HE was present at the beginning of creation (John 1:1), and so no one needed to tell HIM about human nature.

JESUS disrupted the ungodly activities that were taking place at the temple in Jerusalem because it had become a den of robbers and thieves whose greatest sin was that, they were blocking the poor, who couldn't afford their services, from worshiping GOD in the temple during Passover.

Notice how differently JESUS handled those who sold doves (John 2:16). The dove was mostly used by the poor as an acceptable sacrifice for Passover worship, but their product may have been hard for the poor to acquire because of temple admission fees, and the exorbitant money exchanging fees, that were required before the purchase.

JESUS was not protesting against the sacrificial system itself, however, here, the purpose of the sacrifices was being lost to the criminal element. Then too, the merchants were also transacting their business inside the temple in the only area where the Gentiles were permitted to enter, thus, they were also blocking the Gentile's opportunity and right to worship peacefully.

And so, even though the dove merchants were providing a similar temple service for the poor, they were still, in tandem with the other merchants, blocking another segment of GOD's people from worship, in this case, the Gentiles. Here in this passage, JESUS is clearly showing us that GOD will not hold blameless, anyone, who blocks another human being, made in HIS spiritual image, from worshipping HIM, at any time, not in the Christian Church of the first century, and certainly not in the Christian Church today.

WHAT DID WE LEARN FROM CHAPTER TWO?
Here are some key points to remember

(1). "The transformation of water into wine" was the first of JESUS' 35 miracles that are recorded in the four Gospels. (John 2:6-10)

(2). It symbolized that JESUS' ministry would be one of "transformation", specifically, of the human heart and character.

(3). The miracle produced six water pots of wine that were 20 to 30 gallons each. (John 2:6)

(4). JESUS' first miracle was also a sign that HIS ministry would bring joy to man, similar to the joy found at a wedding, because GOD had saved the best for last, which is, JESUS' saving power. (John 2:9-10)

(5). After the wedding JESUS went to Capernaum with HIS mother and brothers for a few days. After this, JESUS seemingly begins to alienate HIMSELF from them, probably because they didn't believe in HIM, and, in fact thought HE was crazy (Mark 3:21, Matthew 4:13, Matthew 12:46-50). (John 2:12)

(6). JESUS disrupted the ungodly activities that were taking place at the temple in Jerusalem because it had become a den of robbers and thieves whose greatest sin was that they were blocking the poor, who couldn't afford their services, from worshiping GOD in the temple during Passover.

CHAPTER THREE:

(13)

JESUS AND NICODEMUS

SCRIPTURE:
The King James Version
(John 3:1-21)

3 **(1)** There was a man of the Pharisees, named Nicodemus, a ruler of the Jews: **(2)** The same came to JESUS by night, and said unto HIM, "RABBI, we know that THOU art a teacher come from GOD: for no man can do these miracles that THOU doest, except GOD be with him". **(3)** JESUS answered and said unto him, "Verily, verily, I say unto thee, except a man be born again, he cannot see the Kingdom of GOD" **(4)** Nicodemus saith unto HIM, "How can a man be born when he is old? Can he enter the second time into his mother's womb, and be born?" **(5)** JESUS answered, "Verily, verily, I say unto thee, Except a man be born of water and of the SPIRIT, he cannot enter into the Kingdom of GOD. **(6)** That which is born of the flesh is flesh; and that which is born of the SPIRIT is spirit. **(7)** Marvel not that I said unto thee, ye must be born again. **(8)** The wind bloweth where it listeth, and thou hearest the sound thereof, but canst not tell whence it cometh, and whither it goeth: so is every one that is born of the SPIRIT." **(9)** Nicodemus answered and said unto HIM, "How can these things be?" **(10)** JESUS answered and said unto him, "Art thou a master of Israel, and knowest not these things? **(11)** Verily, verily, I say unto thee, We speak that we do know, and testify that we have seen; and ye receive not our witness. **(12)** If I have told you earthly things, and ye believe not, how shall ye believe, if I tell you of heavenly things? **(13)** And no man hath ascended up to heaven, but HE that came down from heaven, even the SON of man which is in heaven. **(14)** And as Moses lifted up the serpent in the wilderness, even so must the SON of man be lifted up: **(15)** That whosoever believeth in HIM should not perish, but have eternal life. **(16)** For GOD so loved the world, that HE gave HIS only begotten SON, that whosoever believeth in HIM should not perish, but have everlasting life. **(17)** For GOD sent not HIS SON into the world to condemn the world; but that the world through HIM might be saved. **(18)** He that believeth on HIM is not condemned: but he that believeth not is condemned already, because he hath not believed in the name of the only begotten SON of GOD. **(19)** And this is the condemnation, that light is come into the world, and men loved darkness rather than light, because their deeds were evil. **(20)** For every one that doeth evil hateth the light, neither cometh to the light, lest his deeds should be reproved. (21) But he that doeth truth cometh to the light, that his deeds may be made manifest, that they are wrought in GOD."

COMMENTARY:

Nicodemus was a member of the "Sanhedrin", the ruling council, or, governing body of religion and state under Rome. He was a Pharisee who had zealous dedication to GOD's Law. He was also "a teacher of Israel" and held the distinctive office of being an authoritative interpreter of Scripture. However, he did come to JESUS with an open mind, intent on listening to the Man, WHOM he himself, had seen perform many miracles.

Right away JESUS stuns the seasoned scholar by saying to him, "Except a man be born again, he cannot see the Kingdom of GOD" (John 3:3 - KJV). In other words, JESUS was telling a man who was thought to be spiritual by everyone, including his own self, that, before any spiritual questions can be dealt with, a man must be born anew, spiritually. He would have to be baptized in the SPIRIT that JESUS HIMSELF would later impart (in the person of the HOLY SPIRIT) to anyone that believes in HIM. And even though the concept of a "spiritual rebirth" is clearly evident in the Old Testament, here, Nicodemus is still, clearly confused by this divine revelation of truth (John 3:4).

JESUS further elaborates on HIS prior statement regarding spiritual rebirth in verses 5-7, by stating, "The truth is, no one can enter the Kingdom of GOD without being born of water, and, the SPIRIT". Humans can reproduce only human life, but the HOLY SPIRIT gives new life from Heaven" (NLT). In other words, JESUS is saying that, the first requirement for a person to be eligible for the kingdom of GOD is that GOD has to allow that person to exist in the first place. When a woman's "water" breaks after the fullness of the time of her pregnancy, a person, or persons are born into the world and human life begins its journey in earnest in the physical world. However, only through accepting CHRIST JESUS, first with our lips, and then, in our hearts, (and thereby, inviting the HOLY SPIRIT to dwell within us), can a person ever receive a new spiritual, eternal life in Heaven.

To be "born again" is the phrase that clearly describes the goal of the aspiring Christian. It is the true Christian's desire, that GOD will exact HIS divine power upon our lives with a "moral infusion" that will transform us into a people that can, at all times, reflect HIS image to others, through our own behavior. And just as "Natural Birth" marks the beginning of our new life in the physical world, and makes us "children of man", "Spiritual Birth" marks the beginning of our new life in CHRIST JESUS, and makes us "children of GOD" (John 3:5-6).

At this time, JESUS responds with a question of HIS OWN, by asking Nicodemus, "Art thou a master of Israel, and knowest not these thing (v. 10 – KJV)? In other words, HE was asking him, "aren't you a respected Jewish teacher and yet you don't understand these things?" If you don't believe the things that GOD is doing on earth, you can't possibly believe the things that are done in Heaven" (John 3:10-12).

Then, after giving Nicodemus a prophetic revelation of how HIS earthly ministry would end (Verses 13-15), JESUS goes on to utter what is, arguably, the most well known verse in all of Scripture, when HE states, "For GOD so loved the world, that HE gave HIS only begotten SON, that whosoever believeth in HIM should not perish, but have everlasting life" (John 3:16 - KJV).

It is "the statement" in Scripture that, perhaps, more clearly than all other statements, reveals to us that "GOD's motivation towards HIS people is "love". It is a love that is not limited to a few, or, just to a single group of people. GOD's gifts of Love and Salvation are for everyone who dares to believe. GOD's purpose in sending HIS OWN SON (HIS first advent) is for our "Salvation", and not for our "condemnation". In fact, there is no judgment awaiting those who believe.

The "lost sinners" are those who do not accept CHRIST JESUS as their LORD and SAVIOR, and by rejecting HIM, they already stand condemned. They will remain lost, unless they put their trust and faith in CHRIST JESUS, while they yet live (v. 18). The Scriptures tell us that their judgment is based on this fact: "the LIGHT from Heaven came into the world, but they loved the darkness more than the LIGHT, for their actions were evil. They hate the LIGHT because they want to sin in the darkness. They stay away from the LIGHT for fear their sins will be exposed and they will be punished. But those who desire to do what is right come to the LIGHT gladly, so everyone can see that they are doing what GOD wants" (Vs. 19-21 - NLT).

JOHN THE BAPTIST'S FINAL EXALTATION OF JESUS
(John 3:22-36)

3 (22) After these things came JESUS and HIS disciples into the land of Judaea; and there HE tarried with them and baptized. (23) And John was also baptizing in Aenon near Salim, because there was much water there: and they came, and were baptized. (24) For John was not yet cast into prison. (25) Then there arose a question between some of John's disciples and the Jews about purifying. (26) And they came unto John, and said unto him, "Rabbi, HE that was with thee beyond Jordan, to WHOM thou barest witness, behold, the same baptizeth, and all men come to HIM." (27) John answered and said, "A man can receive nothing, except it be given him from Heaven. (28) Ye yourselves bear me witness, that I said, I am not the CHRIST, but that I am sent before HIM. (29) He that hath the bride is the bridegroom: but the friend of the bridegroom, which standeth and heareth him, rejoiceth greatly because of the bridegroom's voice; this my joy therefore is fulfilled. (30) HE must increase, but I must decrease. (31) HE that cometh from above is above all: he that is of the earth is earthly, and speaketh of the earth: HE that cometh from Heaven is above all. (32) And what HE hath seen and heard, that HE testifieth; and no man receiveth HIS testimony. (33) He that hath received HIS testimony hath set to his seal that GOD is true. (34) For HE WHOM GOD hath sent speaketh the words of GOD: for GOD giveth not the SPIRIT by measure unto HIM. (35) The FATHER loveth the SON, and hath given all things into HIS hand. (36) He that believeth on the SON hath everlasting life: and he that believeth not the SON shall not see life; but the wrath of GOD abideth on HIM.

COMMENTARY:

John chapter 3, verses 22-36, contains, what turned out to be John the Baptist's final testimony of CHRIST JESUS in recorded Scripture. After JESUS and HIS disciples left Jerusalem, they stayed in Judea for a while and baptized there. During that time, John the Baptist was baptizing in Aenon, near Salim, because there was plenty of water there and, also, because there was a continued stream of people seeking to be baptized. This all occurred before John's final incarceration and ultimate beheading at the hands of King Herod Antipas, Herodias, his wife, and, Herodias' daughter of the same name (Mark 6:27-29).

At that time, a certain Jewish man started an argument with one of John's disciples regarding ceremonial cleansing. John's disciple then came to him and informed him that JESUS was baptizing people on the other side of the Jordan River, and that, most of the people were going to HIM to be baptized, instead of coming to them. For a brief space in time, John's ministry had overlapped that of JESUS', by GOD's design. But now, John was realizing that his reign, as being the most prominent preacher of the day, was suddenly coming to an end.

The statement that, JESUS baptized, most likely means that JESUS was overseeing the baptisms done by HIS disciples. John's disciples had probably become angry or jealous because they were no longer the main attraction, and that, JESUS had now begun to steal their shine.

The greatness of John the Baptist is perhaps revealed in his response to his dejected disciples, who already knew of his witness to JESUS being the MESSIAH. John tells them, that, "a man can only receive that which is given to him by GOD in Heaven". He also reminded his disciples that they were forgetting an important part of his teaching, as he had clearly always taught that he himself was not the promised MESSIAH, but was merely preparing the way for HIS coming.

In fact, John himself had found his own joy being fulfilled by CHRIST's arrival on the scene. John refers to himself as the "friend of the bridegroom", who found great joy in the bridegroom's success. He clearly understood, that, his ministry should now decrease, while JESUS, WHO is the true MESSIAH, ministry must increase.

JESUS came from Heaven and would teach of Heavenly things, while John, who was of this earth, could only teach with a limited earthly understanding. Everyone who believes JESUS' teachings will ultimately discover GOD's truth in HIS words. For GOD had placed upon HIM, HIS OWN SPIRIT without measure, and, without limitations. And HE has also given HIM power and authority over all things, both on earth, and, in Heaven.

WHAT DID WE LEARN FROM CHAPTER THREE?
Here are some key points to remember

(1). Nicodemus was a Pharisee, who believed JESUS (John 3:1-2)

(2). We must experience a new birth of spiritual awakening before we can see the Kingdom of Heaven (John 3:3)

(3). GOD did not send JESUS into the world to condemn it. HE sent HIM here to save the world, because HE loves us (John 3:16-17).

(4). There is no judgment awaiting those who believe in CHRIST, and those who don't believe have already been judged, because, they don't believe (John 3:18- 21).

(5). A person can only receive that which is given to them by GOD (John 3:27).

(6). Just as John the Baptist prepared the way for JESUS' first advent, so should we, as Christians, prepare the way for HIS second coming.

(7). Believing in JESUS allows us to discover the truth of GOD. HE speaks GOD's word and shares HIS SPIRIT. Those who don't obey JESUS cannot receive eternal life in Heaven. They can only receive the wrath of GOD (John 3:31-36).

CHAPTER FOUR:

JESUS AND THE SAMARITAN WOMAN

SCRIPTURE:
The King James Version
(John 4:1-42)

4 **(1)** When therefore the LORD knew how the Pharisees had heard that JESUS made and baptized more disciples than John, **(2)** (Though JESUS HIMSELF baptized not, but HIS disciples,) **(3)** HE left Judaea, and departed again into Galilee. **(4)** And HE must needs go through Samaria. **(5)** Then cometh HE to a city of Samaria, which is called Sychar, near the parcel of ground that Jacob gave to his son Joseph. **(6)** Now Jacob's well was there. JESUS therefore, being wearied with HIS journey, sat thus on the well: and it was about the sixth hour. **(7)** There cometh a woman of Samaria to draw water: JESUS saith unto her, "Give ME to drink". **(8)** (For HIS disciples were gone away unto the city to buy meat.) **(9)** Then saith the woman of Samaria unto HIM, "How is it that THOU, being a Jew, askest drink of me, which am a woman of Samaria? For the Jews have no dealings with the Samaritans". **(10)** JESUS answered and said unto her, "If thou knewest the gift of GOD, and WHO it is that saith to thee, Give ME to drink; thou wouldest have asked of HIM, and HE would have given thee living water". **(11)** The woman saith unto HIM, "SIR, THOU hast nothing to draw with, and the well is deep: from whence then hast THOU that living water?" **(12)** Art THOU greater than our father Jacob, which gave us the well, and drank thereof himself, and his children, and his cattle?" **(13)** JESUS answered and said unto her, "Whosoever drinketh of this water shall thirst again: **(14)** But whosoever drinketh of the water that I shall give him shall never thirst; but the water that I shall give him shall be in him a well of water springing up into everlasting life." **(15)** The woman said unto him, "SIR, give me this water, that I thirst not, neither come hither to draw." **(16)** JESUS said unto her, "Go, call thy husband, and come hither." **(17)** The woman answered and said, "I have no husband". JESUS said unto her, "Thou hast well said, I have no husband: **(18)** For thou hast had five husbands; and he whom thou now hast is not thy husband: in that saidst thou truly." **(19)** The woman saith unto HIM, "SIR, I perceive that thou art a prophet. **(20)** Our fathers worshipped in this mountain; and YE say, that in Jerusalem is the place where men ought to worship." **(21)** JESUS saith unto her, "Woman, believe ME, the hour cometh, when ye shall neither in this mountain, nor yet at Jerusalem, worship the FATHER. (22) Ye worship ye know not what: we know what we worship: for salvation is of the Jews. (23) But the hour cometh, and now is, when the true worshipers shall the FATHER in spirit and in truth: for the FATHER seeketh such to worship HIM. (24) GOD is a SPIRIT: and they that worship HIM must worship HIM in spirit and in truth." (25) The woman saith unto HIM, "I know that the MESSIAS cometh, which is called CHRIST: when HE is come, HE will tell us all things." (26) JESUS saith unto her, "I that speak unto thee AM HE." (27) And upon this came HIS disciples, and marveled that HE talked with the woman: yet no man said, "What seekest THOU?" or, "Why talkest THOU with her?" (28) The woman then left her water pot, and went her way into the city, and saith to the men, (29) "Come, see a MAN, which told me all things that ever I did: is not this the CHRIST?" (30) Then they went out of the city, and came unto HIM. (31) In the mean while HIS disciples prayed HIM, saying, "MASTER, eat." (32) But HE said unto them, "I have meat to eat that ye know not of". (33) Therefore said the disciples one to another, "Hath any man brought HIM ought to eat?" (34) JESUS saith unto them, "MY meat is to do the will of HIM that sent ME, and to finish HIS work (35) Say not ye, There are yet four months, and then cometh harvest? behold, I say unto you, Lift up your eyes, and look on the fields; for they are white already to harvest. (36) And he that reapeth receiveth wages, and gathereth fruit unto life eternal: that both he that soweth and he that reapeth may rejoice together. (37) And herein is that saying true, One soweth, and the other reapeth. (38) I sent you to reap that whereon ye bestowed no labour: other men laboured, and ye are entered into their labours." (39) And many of the Samaritans of that city believed on HIM for the saying of the woman, which testified, "HE told me all that I ever did". (40) So when the Samaritans were come unto HIM, they besought HIM that HE would tarry with them: and HE abode there two days. (41) And many more believed because of HIS OWN word; (42) And said unto the woman, "Now we believe, not because of thy saying: for we have heard HIM ourselves, and know that this is indeed the CHRIST, the SAVIOUR of the world".

COMMENTARY:

In the Greek, the word New Testament writers use for "longsuffering" is "makrothumia" (mak-roth-oo-mee-ah). It describes a spirit that never grows irritated, never despairs, and never regards anyone as being beyond salvation. In the Gospel according to Saint John, in chapter 4, verses 1-42, the author of GOD writes of JESUS' journey alone, into Samaria, a land that was rarely, if ever, traveled through by the Jews in those days. HE and HIS Disciples had left Judea together after HIS Disciples had done some baptizing there, and were heading back to Galilee. On the way, JESUS sent HIS Disciples to get food, and HE HIMSELF, continued on into the Samaritan village of Sychar, in the vicinity of the land that Jacob had willed to his son Joseph (Gen. 48:21-22). It was also where Jacob's well is located.

In verse 4 of this passage, the Apostle John tells us that JESUS "had to" go through Samaria, even though we know that there was an alternate, more frequently traveled route that the Jews would take, just east of the Jordan River, through neighboring Perea.

The Jews hated the Samaritans, and the Samaritans did not like the Jews. They had harbored ill-feelings towards each other since the days when the Assyrians, under the rule of King Shalamaneser, defeated Israel and King Hoshea, Israel's last GODly king. The Assyrians took over the capital city of Samaria, and exiled the Israelites to Assyria (2 Kings 17).

The Assyrians then replaced the Israelites with groups of people from Babylon, Cuthah, Avva, Hamath, and Sepharvaim, and resettled them in Samaria and various other towns throughout Israel. The descendants of the Jews, who married and mixed with those Assyrian groups, became the hated Samaritans of JESUS' day.

While these Samaritans were worshipers of the same GOD as the Israelites, they continued to worship at Mount Gerizim, where Moses, Joshua, and the Jews worshiped (Deut. 27:12 & Josh. 8:33) prior to coming to the "promised land". However, since the time after King David moved the worship center to Jerusalem, the "pure breed" Jew's had been worshiping there. The Samaritans were hated simply because they were "half breed" Jews, and thus, no better than Gentiles in the minds of the pure-breed Jews.

However, we see in verse 12 that the woman JESUS encountered at "Jacob's well", still considers Jacob as her forefather, and claims her Jewish heritage. What we see here in John chapter 4, is an attempt by JESUS, to show HIS Disciples, and the world, including future generations, that, the new Gospel that HE preached would be embraced by both Jews and Gentiles alike. HE sought to show that prayer is made for all men, regardless of race, and that, for the coming "Christian Way", there would be no such thing as an enemy, except satan, in all the world. No one would be left outside of the love of CHRIST, and no one has ever been outside of the purpose of GOD. GOD wishes all mankind to be saved.

We also see in this passage, JESUS introducing us to "The Five Laws of Persuasion";

- "Attention" (Vs. 7-9)
- "Interest" (Vs. 10-12)
- "Desire" (Vs. 13-15),
- "Conviction" (Vs. 16-18)
- "Commitment" (Vs. 28-29)

The Samaritan woman that JESUS met at the well that day, like many of us, thirsted and longed for that thing in her life, that she felt was lacking. She had drank from the wells of many men, five husbands, to be exact, and was currently "shacking up" with yet another man when she finally had this surprising and unexpected, life-changing encounter with JESUS.

The Disciples returned just as the woman was leaving, and they were puzzled as to why JESUS was even talking to a woman alone, and they were, perhaps, even more disturbed that the woman was a Samaritan. JESUS had broken many life-changing barriers by venturing into Samaritan territory that day, and no doubt his disciple's feet were touching Samaritan soil for the very first time. However, if they were to train to become fishers of men, they would have to first understand that JESUS' offer of salvation would extend to everyone, both to the Jews, and, to the much hated Gentiles and Samaritans.

The woman went eagerly back to Samaria to witness of her life-changing event at Jacob's well, and though she, herself still had many questions, nevertheless, her life had now been jump-started in a new direction. She had come to the well that day, no doubt, filled with shame for living a life that had, to that point, ostracized her from the other women of her community. However, she left the well having a new lease on life that one can only receive by coming to the end of one's self, and coming face to face with CHRIST JESUS.

It seems as if GOD has placed this longing and thirst, inside of each of us, innately from birth, and the only way to satisfy that longing or thirst, is by seeking, and ultimately finding HIM. It is for the purpose of GOD that man was ever created in first place. And just as no man has ever created anything that was not for his own purpose or benefit, so it is with GOD. Man was created to serve GOD, and until we grasp and understand that, we'll just continue to meander around, searching for physical answers, to problems, that have always been spiritual.

THE HEALING OF THE GOVERNMENT OFFICIAL'S SON
(John 4:43-54)

4 (43) Now after two days HE departed thence, and went into Galilee. (44) For JESUS HIMSELF testified, that a prophet hath no honour in his own country. (45) Then when HE was come into Galilee, the Galilaeans received HIM, having seen all the things that HE did at Jerusalem at the feast: for they also went unto the feast. (46) So JESUS came again into Cana of Galilee, where HE made the water wine. And there was a certain nobleman, whose son was sick at Capernaum. (47) When he heard that JESUS was come out of Judaea into Galilee, he went unto HIM, and besought HIM that HE would come down, and heal his son: for he was at the point of death. (48) Then said JESUS unto him, "Except ye see signs and wonders, ye will not believe." (49) The nobleman saith unto HIM, "SIR, come down ere my child die". (50) JESUS saith unto him, "Go thy way, thy son liveth". And the man believed the word that JESUS had spoken unto him, and he went his way. (51) And as he was now going down, his servants met him, and told him, saying, "Thy son liveth". (52) Then enquired he of them the hour when he began to amend. And they said unto him, "Yesterday at the seventh hour the fever left him". (53) So the father knew that it was at the same hour, in the which JESUS said unto him, "Thy son liveth": and himself believed, and his whole house. (54) This is again the second miracle that JESUS did, when HE was come out of Judaea into Galilee.

COMMENTARY:

JESUS lingered there in Samaria for a couple of days and then continued on north to Galilee with HIS disciples. HE had already pointed out earlier how a prophet is often honored everywhere except his own home country. This proverbial saying, which is also mentioned by the Gospel writers, Matthew (Matt. 13:57) and Mark (Mark 6:4), is re-iterated here by the Apostle John (v. 44). Whether or not JESUS was talking about HIS earthly home country of Galilee or HIS beloved nation of Israel is unclear.

Here, John seems to be preparing his readers for the upcoming rejection of JESUS' doctrine, by even HIS OWN native Jewish people, during HIS three-year mission, here on earth. And even though they had been impressed with HIS miracles and wise speech, ultimately they were a part of the angry mob that killed HIM on Calvary. Their enthusiasm for the GOD WHO healed them was not always indicative of the faith, or lack thereof, that, they had in HIM.

There was a certain royal official with an ailing son, who had made the 25-mile trip from Capernaum hoping to meet JESUS when HE arrived in Cana. The tiny village of Cana was the site of JESUS' first recorded miracle, where HE transformed several barrels of water into wine. Obviously, neither the official's position, nor, his money, was enough to save his son who was now near death back in Capernaum.

The official soon found JESUS and began begging HIM to come to Capernaum and heal his son. JESUS asked the desperate official, who was probably of Jewish descent, "Must I do miraculous signs and wonders before you people will believe in ME?" Without receiving a response from the man, JESUS told him to "Go back home, your son will live". The man believed JESUS and started on his way back home.

While he was in route back to Capernaum, he was met by a few of his servants. They informed the official that his son had made a miraculous recovery at around one o'clock the previous afternoon. When the official heard the time that was given to him by his servants, he knew that it was JESUS, WHO had healed his son. This was the second miracle that JESUS had performed in Galilee, after coming from Judea. From that day on, the official and his entire household became followers of CHRIST JESUS.

WHAT DID WE LEARN FROM CHAPTER FOUR?
Here are some key points to remember

(1). In the story of the Samaritan woman, we learned about "the five laws of persuasion": Attention (Vs. 7-9), Interest (Vs. 10-12), Desire (Vs. 13-15), Conviction (Vs. 16-18), and Commitment (Vs. 28-29).

(2). When evangelizing to win others over to CHRIST, emulate HIM by using these five laws; Ask yourself these questions:
(a). Did I get their attention?
(b). Did I hold their interest?
(c). Did I create a desire to know CHRIST better?
(d). Was the person convicted of their sins?
(e). Did I confront the person clearly with the need to make a decision for CHRIST?

(3). The story of JESUS and the Samaritan Woman proves that, when people know what GOD is willing to do for them for free, then they are able to face their sins, repent, and begin seeking the LORD with their whole heart (v.10).

(4). Our sin shows that our need for GOD is real, and that our problems are spiritual, not physical.

(5). Sin is not threatening when the sinner realizes that punishment is not an issue. GOD is seeking worshipers, and is not looking for new ways to judge us. When the woman was forced to face the living CHRIST, she had to make a decision to either accept or reject HIM (v.17-30).

(6). When we cut through all of the theology, only one issue remains: Do we accept JESUS at HIS word (v.20-30)?

(7). The Good news of CHRIST sets off a chain reaction (v.39 & 53).

CHAPTER FIVE:

THE THIRD SIGN OF THE MESSIAH

SCRIPTURE:
The King James Version
(John 5:1-15)

5 **(1)** After this there was a feast of the Jews; and JESUS went up to Jerusalem. **(2)** Now there is at Jerusalem by the sheep market a pool, which is called in the Hebrew tongue Bethesda, having porches. **(3)** In these lay a great multitude of impotent folk, of blind, halt, withered, waiting for the moving of the water. **(4)** For an angel went down at a certain season into the pool, and troubled the water: whosoever then first after the troubling of the water stepped in was made whole of whatsoever disease he had. **(5)** And a certain man was there, which had an infirmity thirty and eight years. **(6)** When JESUS saw him lie, and knew that he had been now a long time in that case, HE saith unto him, "Wilt thou be made whole?" **(7)** The impotent man answered HIM, "SIR, I have no man, when the water is troubled, to put me into the pool: but while I am coming, another steppeth down before me." **(8)** JESUS saith unto him, "Rise, take up thy bed, and walk." **(9)** And immediately the man was made whole, and took up his bed, and walked: and on the same day was the Sabbath. **(10)** The Jews therefore said unto him that was cured, "It is the Sabbath day: it is not lawful for thee to carry thy bed." **(11)** He answered them, "HE that made me whole, THE SAME said unto me, "Take up thy bed, and walk." **(12)** Then they asked him, "What man is that which said unto thee, "Take up thy bed, and walk?" **(13)** And HE that was healed wist not WHO it was: for JESUS had conveyed HIMSELF away, a multitude being in that place. **(14)** Afterward JESUS findeth him in the temple, and said unto him, "Behold, thou art made whole: sin no more, lest a worse thing come unto thee. **(15)** The man departed, and told the Jews that it was JESUS, which had made him whole.

COMMENTARY:

After JESUS left Galilee, HE returned to Jerusalem to attend an "unnamed" Jewish feast. Just to the north of the temple area, near the "Sheep Gate", was a "double pool" (two pools side by side) called the "Pool of Bethesda". The pool had five covered porches, where the sick, blind, lame, and paralyzed people would come and lay awaiting to be healed by the water.

In those days, the people superstitiously believed that, periodically, an angel would come down from Heaven and stir the water, and afterwards, the first person entering the pool would be healed of their physical afflictions. This event, mentioned in John 5:3b-4 is not found in any existing Greek manuscript dated before A.D. 400. In fact, nowhere in the Bible is this kind of superstition taught, as this verse presents to us, the picture of an act of cruelty by GOD against the sick and the afflicted.

It is believed that this verse was added long after John wrote his Gospel, in order to enlighten the reader as to why the sick and afflicted where assembling by the pool on this occasion. Most modern versions of scripture, including the NIV, and NLT understandably omit this verse.

Anyway, there was a certain man lying on a mat on one of the porches, who had been suffering from an unnamed infirmity for thirty-eight years. When JESUS saw the man HE knew exactly how long he had been ailing. HE asked the man, "Do you want to get well?" The man confirms his own superstition, by replying that he was unable to get to the pool first, because of his condition, and since there was no one to help him, he kept getting beat to the water by others all those years. In other words, he felt like his own physical condition prevented him from being able to get help from GOD, to better his physical condition.

It is a sad commentary as to how living a superstitious life can hinder a person from GOD's blessings. Even today we have our own modern-day superstitions, such as horoscopes, magic eight balls, black-eyed peas kept in our pocket, or eaten on New Year's Day for good luck, seven years bad luck for breaking a mirror, or "send this e-mail to ten people and you will be blessed", etc. Here in this passage (John 5:1-15), JESUS uses this occasion to dispel all such superstition, and HE also sought to put an end to any concept of a superstitious worship of GOD, or mixing the blessings of GOD, with the satanic beliefs of the occult.

This passage is also unique, in the sense that, here, we see JESUS healing a person who had not exhibited any prior faith in HIM. HE simply instructs the man to "Pick up your bed and start walking". Here we see GOD working directly in, and through, HIS "word of command". JESUS is showing here that HIS power is not mere "superstition", but rather, it is "supernatural". This is a case where the long atrophied muscles of a lame man were clearly and instantly made operable. This was the third public miracle that JESUS performed, as a sign that the MESSIAH had come, and that, indeed, HE, HIMSELF, is the long-awaited MESSIAH.

JESUS CLAIMS TO BE THE SON OF GOD
(John 5:16-30)

5 (16) And therefore did the Jews persecute JESUS, and sought to slay HIM, because HE had done these things on the Sabbath day. **(17)** But JESUS answered them, "MY FATHER worketh hitherto, and I work." **(18)** Therefore the Jews sought the more to kill HIM, because HE not only had broken the Sabbath, but said also that GOD was HIS FATHER, making HIMSELF equal to GOD. **(19)** Then answered JESUS and said unto them, "Verily, verily, I say unto you, the SON can do nothing of HIMSELF, but what HE seeth the FATHER do: for what things soever HE doeth, these also doeth the SON likewise. **(20)** For the FATHER loveth the SON, and sheweth HIM all things that HIMSELF doeth: and HE will shew HIM greater works than these, that ye may marvel. **(21)** For as the FATHER raiseth up the dead, and quickeneth them; even so the SON quickeneth whom HE will. **(22)** For the FATHER judgeth no man, but hath committed all judgment unto the SON: **(23)** That all men should honour the SON, even as they honour the FATHER. He that honoureth not the SON honoureth not the FATHER which hath sent HIM. **(24)** Verily, verily, I say unto you, he that heareth MY word, and believeth on HIM that sent ME, hath everlasting life, and not come into condemnation; but is passed from death unto life. **(25)** Verily, verily, I say unto you, the hour is coming, and now is, when the dead shall hear the voice of the SON of GOD: and they that hear shall live. **(26)** For the FATHER hath life in HIMSELF: so hath HE given to the SON to have life in HIMSELF; **(27)** And hath given HIM authority to execute judgment also, because HE is the SON of man. **(28)** Marvel not at this: for the hour is coming, in the which all that are in the graves shall hear HIS voice, **(29)** And shall come forth; they that have done good, unto the resurrection of life; and they that have done evil, unto the resurrection of damnation. **(30)** I can of MINE OWN SELF do nothing: as I hear, I judge: and MY judgment is just; because I seek not MY OWN will, but the will of the FATHER which hath sent ME."

COMMENTARY:

John chapter 5 is one of the New Testament's most basic passages on the subject of "Eternal Life". Eternal Life is more than just endless, and it has a quality and character that is distinctly its own. It is GOD's OWN life, infused with HIS OWN vitality and moral character, and it is given to us, upon our own "spiritual rebirth".

Everyone who undergoes this "born again" experience, and receives this new life, can begin to have fellowship with GOD, and, with other believers. We become linked with GOD, and one another, by way of an eternal bond that can never be broken.

When we possess eternal life, it manifests itself in our love and behavior towards GOD, and, towards one another. Our heritage with death is broken by the vicarious sacrifice of JESUS on the cross at Golgotha, and we are given the power of the HOLY SPIRIT to flow through us, and help transform us into a spiritual body that desires right living, or a longing to be more like CHRIST JESUS. The Apostle John's portrait of JESUS is perhaps, the most theological of the four Gospels. He begins his account by presenting JESUS, as ONE WHO existed with GOD, and as GOD, from the beginning, before creation.

In the New Testament Greek, the word used for "believe" is "pisteuo" (pist-yoo-o), and it means "to have faith in, or commit to trust in". It is the key word in John's Gospel account, as it is used no fewer than 98 times. In so many words, John's writing style quite literally confronts us with the concept of a deep necessity to believe in CHRIST JESUS as the SON of the LIVING GOD. A study of John's unique portrait of CHRIST can serve to enrich our lives with faith in JESUS, and enable us to walk more closely in HIS will, and, in HIS ways.

John 5:16-30 is the first half of what is now known as "The Discourse" (verses 16-47). It is one of the more vivid passages in Scripture, where JESUS claims to be GOD, or equal with GOD. Here in this passage, JESUS claims to be equal with GOD in three ways;

- First of all, HE claims to be equal with GOD in "Works" (vv. 17-21 & 25). There we find an angry mob of religious leaders ready to kill HIM, because HE had, once again, healed a man on the Sabbath. JESUS responds by telling them that HE, like HIS FATHER GOD, never stops working, and, in addition, HE also has the power to even raise from the dead, anyone HE wants to, just like HIS FATHER GOD.

- Secondly, HE claims to have been given equality with GOD in executing "Judgment" (vv. 22 & 27-30). At that time, the Jews widely believed that GOD HIMSELF, would judge all men. But here in this passage JESUS contends that it is indeed HE, WHO will judge by direction of HIS FATHER GOD.

- And thirdly, JESUS claims to be given equality with GOD in "Honor" (v. 23). Here HE tells the religious leaders that everyone will honor HIM, just as

- they honor HIS FATHER GOD, and anyone who refuses to honor HIM, is also refusing to honor HIS FATHER GOD, WHO sent HIM.

JESUS spoke boldly and authoritatively to the hardhearted religious leaders of HIS day, during HIS three-year ministry, here on earth. And sadly, because of that hardheartedness, they could not bring themselves to believe HIS message of the New Covenant, which HE would very shortly, sign with HIS OWN blood. We as individuals, must personally come into harmony with the reality of JESUS' message, and then, recognize the authority that HE has over us, and all creation. For JESUS truly is the SON of the LIVING GOD, and with all power, HE has risen to the throne, from which HE will judge all mankind, at the appointed time of HIS FATHER GOD.

WITNESSES TO JESUS
(John 5:31-47)

5 (31) "If I bear witness to MYSELF, MY witness is not true. (32) There is another that beareth witness of ME; and I know that the witness which he witnesseth of ME is true. (33) Ye sent unto John, and he bare witness unto the truth. (34) But I receive not testimony from man: but these things I say, that ye might be saved. (35) He was a burning and shining light: and ye were willing for a season to rejoice in his light. (36) But I have greater witness than that of John: for the works which the FATHER hath given ME to finish, the same works that I do, bear witness of ME, that the FATHER hath sent ME. (37) And the FATHER HIMSELF, which hath sent ME, hath borne witness of ME. Ye have neither heard HIS voice at any time, nor seen HIS shape. (38) And ye have not HIS word abiding in you: for WHOM HE hath sent, HIM ye believe not. (39) Search the Scriptures; for in them ye think ye have eternal life: and they are they which testify of ME. (40) And ye will not come to ME, that ye may have life. (41) I receive not honour from men. (42) But I know you, that you have not the love of GOD in you. (43) I am come in MY FATHER's name, and ye receive ME not: if another shall come in his own name, him ye will receive. (44) How can ye believe, which receive honour one of another, and seek not the honour that cometh from GOD only? (45) Do not think that I will accuse you to the FATHER: there is one that will accuseth you, even Moses, in whom ye trust. (46) For had ye believed Moses, ye would have believed ME: for he wrote of ME. (47) But if ye believe not his writings, how shall ye believe MY words?"

COMMENTARY:

In the second half of JESUS' discourse to the Jewish religious leaders at Jerusalem, HE shifts HIS thoughts from that of HIS unity with GOD the FATHER, to that of those, who bear witness of HIM, including John the Baptist, Moses, and even GOD HIMSELF.

JESUS states that if HE bore witness of HIMSELF, that, as far as HIS Pharisee audience was concerned, HIS testimony would not be valid. They would only consider that to be an arrogant claim of self-exaltation. So HE, instead, points first, to the witness of John the Baptist, which they themselves, had already heard and rejoiced about.

HE then speaks of a greater witness, HIS teachings and miracles, which were assigned to HIM by GOD HIMSELF, WHOM sent HIM. HE tells also how GOD has testified of HIM, but they were unable to see, or hear HIM, because HIS message is not in their hearts. If the FATHER's message were in their hearts, then, they would also believe HIM.

JESUS then invited them to search the Scriptures, which they believe, gives them eternal life, and even they who wrote the Scriptures, write of HIM. HE tells them that they are so busy honoring themselves that they can't recognize the honor that comes from GOD alone. And so, in the end, those same Pharisees who claimed that they believed Moses, would actually be condemned by Moses, because they had actually failed to recognize the very PERSON WHOM Moses wrote about.

JESUS tells them, however, that their approval or disapproval means nothing to HIM, because they don't have the love of GOD in them. HE came representing the FATHER and they rejected HIM, while readily accepting those, who represent themselves. Anyone who can't believe the word of GOD, as it is written, by HIS assigned authors, can't believe in JESUS CHRIST the SAVIOR either.

WHAT DID WE LEARN FROM CHAPTER FIVE?
Here are some key points to remember

(1). Sometimes we don't want to be healed, because healing will turn responsibility for our lives and behavior, over to us. (John 5:6-7)

(2). It is much wiser to obey GOD, than to obey those who try to tell you what to do, but neither care about you, nor, are able to help you. (John 5:11-13)

(3). JESUS is equal to GOD in works. (John 5:19-21, 25-28)

(4). JESUS is equal to GOD in judgment. (John 5:22, 30)

(5). JESUS is equal to GOD in honor. (John 5:22-23)

(6). GOD is JESUS' greatest witness. (John 5:36-37)

(7). Moses bore witness for JESUS. (John 5:45-47) (Genesis 3:15, 22:18, 49:10) (Numbers 24:17) (Deuteronomy 18:15)

CHAPTER SIX:

JESUS FEEDS THE FIVE THOUSAND

SCRIPTURE:
The King James Version
(John 6:1-15)

6 (1) After these things JESUS went over the Sea of Galilee, which is the sea of Tiberias. (2) And a great multitude followed HIM, because they saw HIS miracles which HE did on them that were diseased. (3) And JESUS went up into a mountain, and there HE sat with HIS disciples. (4) And the Passover, a feast of the Jews, was nigh. (5) When JESUS lifted up HIS eyes, and saw a great company come unto HIM, HE saith unto Philip, "Whence shall we buy bread, that these may eat?" (6) And this HE said to prove him: for HE knew what HE would do. (7) Philip answered HIM, "Two hundred pennyworth of bread is not sufficient for them, that every one of them may take a little." (8) One of HIS disciples, Andrew, Simon Peter's brother, saith unto HIM, (9) "There is a lad here, which hath five barley loaves, and two small fishes: but what are they among so many?" (10) And JESUS said, "Make the men sit down." Now there was much grass in the place. So the men sat down, in number about five thousand. (11) And JESUS took the loaves; and when HE had given thanks, HE distributed to the disciples, and the disciples to them that were set down; and likewise of the fishes as much as they would. (12) When they were filled, HE said unto HIS disciples, "Gather up the fragments that remain, that nothing be lost." (13) Therefore they gathered them together, and filled twelve baskets with fragments of the five barley loaves, which remained over and above unto them that had eaten. (14) Then those men, when they had seen the miracle that JESUS did, said, "This is of a truth that prophet that should come into the world. (15) When JESUS therefore perceived that they would come and take HIM by force, to make HIM a king, HE departed again into a mountain HIMSELF alone.

COMMENTARY:

JESUS' feeding of the five thousand men, plus women and children, along with HIS spectacular resurrection, are the only miracles of JESUS, that are mentioned by all four Gospel writers. This legendary feeding took place late in the afternoon, one day, on the slopes of a mountain, and not far from the banks of the Sea of

Galilee, which is otherwise known as the Sea of Tiberias. It was near the tiny village of Bethsaida, the home of Philip, Andrew, Peter, and probably Nathaniel, four of JESUS' original disciples. This event can also be referenced in the Gospels of Matthew (14:13-21), Mark (6:30-44), and Luke (9:10-17).

JESUS, WHO is the ultimate, perpetual teacher of man, is always busy testing and refining our faith. And here in this sixth chapter of this Gospel account of John, HE gives us yet another vivid example of just such a test of faith. Philip, being one of the disciples, whom was a native of Bethsaida, is chosen by JESUS to set up this particular lesson in "trusting GOD's provision".

In verse five, JESUS asks Philip, where they could buy food to feed all these people. First of all, John tells us that JESUS already knew how Philip would respond (V. 6). Philip says to JESUS that it would take a small fortune to feed this many people (V. 7). In other words, Philip was openly admitting to "the human impossibility" of the situation JESUS sought to address.

GOD always wants us to trust in HIS unique sovereign ability to do all things, and we see here in this passage, that, even if such a large amount of bread were available, they still would not have had the amount of money it would have taken to purchase it. Andrew, who had gone into the crowd to try and determine the amount of food already available, then, steps forward to report that the only food available was that of a little lad's lunch, which were five barley loaves and two fish (Vs. 8-9).

With all of man's efforts now exhausted, the stage was set for JESUS to once again demonstrate HIS compassion and power. As the GOOD SHEPHERD, JESUS instructs HIS sheep to sit on the grassy slopes. Then, HE took the loaves from the little boy's lunch, raised them up and gave thanks to GOD. HE then passes the loaves to HIS disciples to distribute to the crowd. Afterwards, HE did the same with the fish, and they all ate until they were full. JESUS then instructs HIS disciples to gather up the leftovers so that nothing would be wasted, and the amount collected filled twelve baskets.

It was an event reminiscent of when GOD had fed the Israelites in the wilderness, with manna from Heaven, through Moses. They also recalled Moses' prophesy of a coming PROPHET, who would be like him (Deuteronomy 18:15), and that HE would be the ONE that they should listen to. And when the people recognized this sign, they sought to make JESUS their king.

This miracle, just like all the others, was an attempt by JESUS, to appeal to the spiritual ignorance of HIS people. And, although the twelve disciples were closer to JESUS, than any of the other people present, they too, at this point, were still lingering in spiritual blindness. The feeding of the five thousand men, plus women and children, was the fourth sign of the MESSIAH.

JESUS WALKS ON WATER
(John 6:16-21)

6 **(16)** And when even was now come, HIS disciples went down unto the sea. **(17)** And entered into a ship, and went over the sea toward Capernaum. And it was now dark, and JESUS was not come to them. **(18)** And the sea arose by reason of a great wind that blew. **(19)** So when they had rowed about five and twenty or thirty furlongs, they see JESUS walking on the sea, and drawing nigh unto the ship: and they were afraid. **(20)** But HE saith unto them, "It is I; be not afraid." **(21)** Then they willingly received HIM into the ship: and immediately the ship was at the land whither they went.

COMMENTARY:

On the evening of the miraculous feeding, JESUS' disciples went down to the shore of the Sea of Galilee to wait for JESUS to disburse the crowd. However, as darkness fell, and JESUS had not yet come, they decided to get into the boat and head on across the water to Capernaum without HIM.

After they had gone three or four miles, which is about half way across the tiny sea, they were besieged by a storm and high winds. Caught in the open sea, they found themselves straining with the oars trying to keep control of the boat. The Sea of Galilee is noted for its sudden and severe storms. All of a sudden the frightened disciples see a shadowy figure coming towards them, walking upon the water. It was JESUS, and HE said to them "It is I, don't be afraid".

This fifth sign of the MESSIAH serves to show us how JESUS, quite literally, comes to us from across the storms of life, with HIS hands stretched out to save, and HE speaks in a calm, clear voice, and HE bids us to "Have no fear". "Be of good cheer", and "Be not afraid" is what JESUS often said to HIS disciples, but it is also a statement that is directed to anyone who chooses to put their faith in HIS saving hand, even to those in this day and age.

We must trust JESUS, that, HE will save us from our troubles, and deliver us into the safety of HIS eternal peace, and we must never leave home without HIM, as the disciples did in this instance, but rather, we must always carry HIM, deeply within our hearts, wherever and whenever we go.

THE BREAD OF LIFE
(John 6:22-59)

6 **(22)** The day following, when the people which stood on the other side of the sea saw that there was none other boat there, save that one whereinto HIS disciples were entered, and that JESUS went not with HIS disciples into the boat, but that HIS disciples were gone away alone; **(23)** (Howbeit there came other boats from Tiberias nigh unto the place where they did eat bread, after that the LORD had given thanks:) **(24)** When the people therefore saw that JESUS was not there, neither HIS disciples, they also took shipping, and came to Capernaum, seeking for JESUS. **(25)** And when they had found HIM on the other side of the sea, they said unto HIM, "RABBI, when camest THOU hither?"

(26) JESUS answered them and said, "Verily, verily, I say unto you, ye seek ME, not because ye saw the miracles, but because ye did eat of the loaves, and were filled. **(27)** Labour not for the meat which perisheth, but for that meat which endureth unto everlasting life, which the SON of man shall give unto you: for HIM hath GOD the FATHER sealed." **(28)** Then said they unto HIM, "What shall we do, that we might work the works of GOD? **(29)** JESUS answered and said unto them, "This is the work of GOD, that ye believe on HIM WHOM HE hath sent." **(30)** They said therefore unto HIM, "What sign shewest THOU then, that we may see, and believe THEE? What dost THOU work? **(31)** Our fathers did eat manna in the desert; as it is written, he gave them bread from Heaven to eat." **(32)** Then JESUS said unto them, "Verily, verily I say unto you, Moses gave you not that bread from Heaven; but MY FATHER giveth you the true bread from Heaven. **(33)** For the bread of GOD is HE which cometh down from Heaven, and giveth life unto the world. **(34)** Then said they unto HIM, LORD, evermore give us this bread. **(35)** And JESUS said unto them, "I am the bread of life: he that cometh to ME shall never thirst. **(36)** But I said unto you, that ye also have seen ME, and believe not. **(37)** All that the FATHER giveth ME shall come to ME; and him that cometh to ME I will no wise cast out. **(38)** For I came down from Heaven, not to do MINE OWN will, but the will of HIM that sent ME. **(39)** And this is the FATHER's will which hath sent ME, that of all which HE hath given ME I should lose nothing, but should raise it up again at the last day. **(40)** And this is the will of HIM that sent ME, that every one which seeth the SON, and believeth on HIM, may have everlasting life: and I will raise HIM up at the last day."

(41) The Jews then murmured at HIM, because HE said, "I AM the bread which came down from Heaven." (42) And they said, "Is not this JESUS, the son of Joseph, whose father and mother we know? How is it then that HE saith, I came down from Heaven? (43) JESUS therefore answered and said unto them, "Murmur not among yourselves. (44) No man can come to ME, except the FATHER which hath sent ME draw him: and I will raise him up at the last day. (45) It is written in the prophets, "And they shall be all taught of GOD". Every man therefore that hath heard, and hath learned of the FATHER, cometh unto ME. (46) Not that any man hath seen the FATHER, save HE which is of GOD, HE hath seen the FATHER. (47) Verily, verily, I say unto you, he that believeth on ME hath everlasting life. (48) I AM the bread of life. (49) Your fathers did eat manna in the wilderness, and are dead. (50) This is the bread which cometh down from Heaven, that a man may eat thereof, and not die. (51) I AM the living bread which came down from Heaven: if any man eat of this bread, he shall live for ever: and the bread that I will give is MY flesh, which I will give for the life of the world." (52) The Jews therefore strove among themselves, saying, "How can this man give us HIS flesh to eat?" (53) Then JESUS said unto them, "Verily, verily, I say unto you, except ye eat the flesh of the SON of man, and drink HIS blood, ye have no life in you. (54) Whoso eateth MY flesh, and drinketh MY blood, hath eternal life; and I will raise HIM up at the last day. (55) For MY flesh is meat indeed, and MY blood is drink indeed. (56) He that eateth MY flesh, and drinketh MY blood, dwelleth in ME, and I in him. (57) As the living FATHER hath sent ME, and I live by the FATHER: so he that eateth ME, even he shall live by ME. (58) This is that bread which came down from Heaven: not as your fathers did eat manna, and are dead: he that eateth of this bread shall live for ever." (59) These things said HE in the synagogue, as HE taught in Capernaum.

COMMENTARY:

Throughout the course of human events men and women make many choices by way of the "freedom of choice" grace gift, which GOD grants to each of us personally. Hopefully, we are wise enough to make one of our choices, the choice of freedom, which we can only find in our LORD and SAVIOR, JESUS CHRIST.
The Gospel of John is the Gospel of the seven great "I AM" statements" of Scripture, that were uttered to various people long ago by CHRIST JESUS, during HIS three-year ministry here on earth.

It must not be forgotten, that, even though those statements were directed to a people who have long since passed away, they are also intended, by GOD, to permeate the hearts (kardia), minds and souls of each generation since. Through CHRIST, GOD makes it possible for every one born into this world to be offered the taste of Salvation.

In John chapter 6, taking up at verse 22, the morning following HIS miraculous "feeding of the five thousand" and HIS legendary "walk on water", crowds of people, who had only heard about the miraculous feeding, begin gathering on shore waiting to see JESUS. They were aware that the disciples had left and went across the lake toward Capernaum without JESUS, but they were unaware that JESUS had later walked across the water to their boat. Several boatloads of them had sailed from Tiberias and landed at the site of the miraculous feeding, but when they realized that JESUS was no longer there, they climbed back into their boats and sailed across the tiny Sea of Galilee to Capernaum to look for HIM there.

When they arrived at Capernaum and found HIM, they questioned HIM as to how HE got there. Ignoring their question, JESUS instead reveals to them that HE knows the true reason why they sought HIM. HE tells them that they sought HIM only because HE fed them the day before, and that it was not because of any other miraculous signs. HE then warns them not to be concerned about "perishable things" like food, but instead, they should spend their energy seeking "the eternal life" that only HE can give them. For GOD had sent HIM to them, for that very purpose, and GOD, wants them to believe in the ONE that HE has sent.

"I AM the BREAD OF LIFE" is what JESUS said to this huge crowd of people, as HE taught in the temple at Capernaum in John 6:35. It is the first of the "Seven Great I AM Statements" that JESUS spoke, during HIS three-year ministry here on earth. And certainly no one who has ever come to JESUS will ever be hungry, or thirst again. JESUS, alone, is able to meet man's need for eternal life.

In the world, there are two very different "perspectives of salvation". The most common is "man's perspective of salvation" which has no validity at all. This occurs when a person walks up to the altar, or stands and raise their hands declaring they want salvation, and then, the preacher or pastor leads them in a prayer, and then, "he, declares them saved".

In John 6:35-59, "GOD's perspective of Salvation", which is the only one that counts, is revealed to us by JESUS. Here JESUS is affirming that HE HIMSELF is the most essential element, or ingredient, needed to provide and sustain spiritual life (complete the process of salvation after professing with the mouth). Physical bread must be eaten and digested before it can become a part of us physically, and in the biblical sense, JESUS (the WORD), must be taken in and digested in order to become a part of us mentally and spiritually.

In John chapter 1, we are told that JESUS is "the WORD" and "the WORD was with GOD", and "the WORD was GOD", and then the Scriptures tell us that the WORD, which is JESUS, became "flesh". We must, by faith, take in JESUS' flesh and blood, which is "the Word and life", completely, before HE can become a part of us, and sustain us, totally. We must mentally and spiritually eat HIS flesh and drink HIS blood, or, in other words, allow "the Word of GOD" to "permeate our heart" (become the way we think and behave), before we can complete the "process" of salvation. JESUS lives by the power of the LIVING FATHER WHO sent HIM to us, and, in the same way, those who partake of the LIVING CHRIST will also live, because of HIM.

In this passage JESUS tells us plainly, over and over again (Vs.37, 43, & 65), that "no one can come to HIM unless GOD the FATHER sends them to HIM, and then HE HIMSELF will raise them up "in the last day" into eternal salvation. In verse 45 JESUS tells us just who will receive salvation, and exactly how GOD the FATHER will select those whom HE will send to the SON. Here HE tells us that all those who are willing to "hear" and "learn" the Word from GOD the HOLY SPIRIT (John 14:15-17 & 23-26) will be allowed to come to HIM by GOD the FATHER. This statement by JESUS lets us know that "there won't be anyone walking around in Heaven who doesn't know GOD", so don't get it twisted.

Since the creation of man, he has always sought and asked for signs from GOD so that he might believe. However, no matter how many signs and miracles GOD has delivered over the centuries, man still has never been able to maintain a trust and belief in GOD for very long. Despite the fact that GOD tells us "it is HIS way or nothing", we continue to use our "human ingenuity" to try to overcome the world. It is a method that even JESUS, WHO was a perfect human being, didn't apply. HE knew that only GOD could direct us through our own, self-imposed mess, and then deliver us safely into HIS OWN glorious presence in the last day. "Human effort accomplishes nothing". Only the HOLY SPIRIT (the SPIRIT) through JESUS (the Word) gives eternal from GOD the FATHER (v.63).

GOD has never asked anything more from us than to show that we have faith in HIM (saving faith), by our actions and behavior. Yet we continue to this day to ask GOD, over and over again, to "prove HIMSELF" with more and more supernatural acts, even though we have never been able to "prove ourselves" to HIM, through "one simple act" of belief and obedience to HIM. And despite HIS continued faithfulness to us, by way of HIS daily provisions, mercy, and salvation, the world's sin continues to be, "unbelief in CHRIST JESUS" (John 16:9).

MANY DISCIPLES DESERT JESUS
(John 6:60-71)

6 (60) Many therefore of HIS disciples, when they had heard this, said, "This is an hard saying; who can hear it?" **(61)** When JESUS knew in HIMSELF that HIS disciples murmured at it, HE said unto them, "Doth this offend you? **(62)** What and if ye see the SON of man ascend up where HE was before? **(63)** It is the SPIRIT that quickeneth; the flesh profiteth nothing: the words that I speak unto you, they are SPIRIT, and they are life. **(64)** But there are some of you that believe not." For JESUS knew from the beginning who they were that believeth not, and who should betray HIM. **(65)** And HE said, "Therefore said I unto you, that no man can come unto ME, except it were given unto him of MY FATHER." **(66)** From that time many of HIS disciples went back, and walked no more with HIM. **(67)** Then said JESUS unto the twelve, "Will ye also go away? **(68)** Then Simon Peter answered HIM, "LORD, to whom shall we go? THOU hast the words of eternal life. **(69)** And we believe and are sure that THOU art that CHRIST, the SON of the LIVING GOD. **(70)** JESUS answered them, "Have not I chosen you twelve, and one of you is a devil?" **(71)** HE spake of Judas Iscariot the son of Simon: for he it was that should betray HIM, being one of the twelve.

COMMENTARY:

The apostle Paul wrote in 1 Corinthians 1:23-24, "But we preach CHRIST crucified, unto the Jews, a stumbling block, and to the Greeks foolishness; But unto them which are called, both Jews and Greeks, CHRIST is the power of GOD, and the wisdom of GOD". What the apostle is saying here is that, when we preach that CHRIST was crucified, the Jews are offended, and the Gentiles say that it is all nonsense. But to those called by GOD to Salvation, both Jews and Gentiles, CHRIST is the mighty power of GOD, and also, the wonderful wisdom of GOD.

In John 6:60-71 we see just such a case of JESUS' truth, and how it can be a stumbling block, or offend those, who can't bring themselves to believe and accept HIS holy words. After JESUS declared that HE was the "true BREAD from

Heaven", even many of HIS OWN disciples found HIM hard to accept. In fact, all but the original twelve turned away and deserted HIM. Then, JESUS turned to the twelve that remained and explained, "This is what I mean when I say that people can't come to ME unless the FATHER brings them to ME".

GOD's word is such that it will draw those who believe, and turn those away, who don't believe. When JESUS asked the twelve remaining disciples if they were going to leave HIM also, the apostle Peter steps forward and makes one of most profound statements of faith in all of Scripture, when he utters, "LORD, to whom would we go? YOU alone have the words that give eternal life. We believe them, and we know you are the CHRIST, the SON of the LIVING GOD". And of the twelve remaining disciples, still, there was one left, whom would ultimately betray HIM.

WHAT DID WE LEARN FROM CHAPTER SIX?
Here are some key points to remember

(1). The feeding of five thousand is mentioned by all four Gospel writers, and is the fourth sign of the MESSIAH.
(2). JESUS feed five thousand men, plus women and children after turning five barley loaves and two fish into enough to feed and fill everyone, and, have twelve baskets of food left over. (John 6:13)
(3). JESUS walked 3-4 miles on the waters of the Sea of Galilee. (John 6:19)
(4). JESUS' miraculous walk on water was the fifth sign that HE was indeed the MESSIAH.
(5). "I AM the BREAD of life" is the first of JESUS' seven great "I AM statements" that are found in the Gospel of John.
(6). All but the original twelve disciples deserted JESUS at Capernaum. (John 6:66-67)
(7). No one can come to JESUS, unless GOD the FATHER draws them to HIM. (John 6:65)

CHAPTER SEVEN:

(42)

JESUS AND HIS BROTHERS

SCRIPTURE:
The King James Version
(John 7:1-9)

7 **(1)** After these things JESUS walked in Galilee: for HE would not walk in Jewry, because the Jews sought to kill HIM. **(2)** Now the Jews' feast of Tabernacles was at hand. **(3)** HIS brethren therefore said unto HIM, "Depart hence, and go into Judaea, that THY disciples also may see the works that THOU doest. **(4)** For there is no man that doeth any thing in secret, and he himself seeketh to be known openly. If THOU do these things, shew THYSELF to the world." **(5)** For neither did HIS brethren believe in HIM. **(6)** Then JESUS said unto them, "MY time is not yet come: but your time is always ready. **(7)** The world cannot hate you; but ME it hateth, because I testify of it, that the works thereof are evil. **(8)** Go ye up unto this feast: I go not up yet unto this feast; for MY time is not yet full come." **(9)** When HE had said these words unto them, HE abode still in Galilee.

COMMENTARY:

After JESUS had taught about HIMSELF being "the bread of life" in the synagogue at Capernaum where most of HIS disciples had deserted HIM, HE dwelled for another six months in HIS homeland of Galilee, going from town to town preaching and teaching the Word. HE stayed away from Judea, because the Jewish leaders there were plotting to kill HIM.

The time for the "Feast of the Tabernacles" had arrived and JESUS' brothers, who didn't believe that HE was the MESSIAH, scoffed at HIM about going into Jerusalem and attending the feast, instead of hiding HIMSELF in Galilee from the Jewish leaders. "YOU can't become a public figure if YOU hide like this" they scoffed. If YOU can do such wonderful things, go to Jerusalem and prove it to the world".

JESUS' brothers, James, Joseph, Simon, and Judas (Matthew 13:55) had no spiritual understanding of their HALF-BROTHER's mission, or GOD's plan for the world through HIM. For, they could only see the human logic of this most divine situation. They thought that JESUS should display HIMSELF in the most powerful way that HE could, but GOD's plan was to show HIM in the humility of the cross.

JESUS TEACHES OPENLY AT THE TEMPLE IN JERUSALEM
(John 7:10-36)

7 **(10)** But when HIS brethren were gone up, then went HE also up unto the feast, not openly, but as it were in secret. **(11)** Then the Jews sought HIM at the feast, and said, "Where is HE?" **(12)** And there was much murmuring among the people concerning HIM: for some said, "HE is a good man: others said, "Nay"; but HE deceiveth the people." **(13)** Howbeit on man spake openly of HIM for fear of the Jews. **(14)** Now about the midst of the feast JESUS went up into the temple, and taught. **(15)** And the Jews marveled, saying, "How knoweth this MAN letters, having never learned? **(16)** JESUS answered them, and said, "MY doctrine is not MINE, but HIS that sent ME. **(17)** If any man will do HIS will, he shall know of the doctrine, whether it be of GOD, or whether I speak of MYSELF. **(18)** He that speaketh of himself seeketh his own glory: but he that seeketh HIS glory that sent him, the same is true, and no unrighteousness is in him. **(19)** Did not Moses give you the law, and yet none of you keepeth the law? Why go ye about to kill ME?" **(20)** The people answered and said, "THOU hast a devil: who goeth about to kill THEE? **(21)** JESUS answered and said unto them, "I have done one work, and ye all marvel. **(22)** Moses therefore gave unto you circumcision; (not because it is of Moses, but of the fathers;) and ye on the Sabbath day circumcise a man. **(23)** If a man on the Sabbath day receive circumcision, that the law of Moses should not be broken; are ye angry at ME, because I have made a man every whit whole on the Sabbath day? **(24)** Judge not according to the appearance, but judge righteous judgment." **(25)** The said one of them of Jerusalem, "Is not this HE, WHOM they seek to kill? **(26)** But, lo, HE speaketh boldly, and they say nothing unto HIM. Do the rulers know indeed that this is the very CHRIST? **(27)** Howbeit we know this MAN whence HE is: but when CHRIST cometh, on man knoweth whence HE is." **(28)** Then cried JESUS in the temple as HE taught, saying, "Ye both know ME, and ye know whence I AM: and I AM not come of MYSELF, but HE that sent ME is true, WHOM ye know not. **(29)** But I know HIM: for I AM from HIM, and HE hath sent ME." **(30)** Then they sought to take HIM: but no man laid hands on HIM, because HIS hour was not yet come. **(31)** And many of the people believed on HIM, and said, "When CHRIST cometh, will HE do more miracles than these which this man hath done?" **(32)** The Pharisees heard that the people murmured such things concerning HIM; and the Pharisees and the chief priests sent officers to take HIM. **(33)** Then said JESUS unto them, "Yet a little while am I with you, and then I go unto HIM that sent ME. **(34)** Ye shall seek ME, and shall not find ME:

and where I AM, thither ye cannot come." (35) Then said the Jews among themselves, "Whither will HE go, that we shall not find HIM? Will HE go unto the dispersed among the Gentiles, and teach the Gentiles? (36) What manner of saying is this that HE said, "Ye shall seek ME, and shall not find ME: and where I AM, thither ye cannot come?"

COMMENTARY:

The time for the "Feast of the Tabernacles" had arrived and JESUS' brothers, who didn't believe that HE was the MESSIAH, scoffed at HIM about going into Jerusalem and attending the feast, instead of hiding HIMSELF in Galilee from the Jewish leaders. "YOU can't become a public figure if YOU hide like this" they scoffed. If YOU can do such wonderful things, go to Jerusalem and prove it to the world".

JESUS' brothers, James, Joseph, Simon, and Judas (Matthew 13:55) had no spiritual understanding of their HALF-BROTHER's mission, or GOD's plan for the world through HIM. For, they could only see the human logic of this most divine situation. They thought that JESUS should display HIMSELF in the most powerful way that HE could, but GOD's plan was to show HIM in the humility of the cross.

The Feast of the Tabernacles was called by the great Jewish historian, Josephus, the Jews holiest and greatest feast. It was called the "feast of ingathering", and was a time of thanksgiving to GOD for their fall harvest. After JESUS' brothers left for Jerusalem, HE soon followed, being careful not to be seen by anyone.

The Jews, of Judaism's religious hierarchy, were asking everyone at the festival if they had seen JESUS, and there was also a lot of discussion concerning JESUS among the throngs of people, who had gathered there. They had mixed opinions about the ONE WHO claimed to be the SON of GOD and MESSIAH. Some believed HIM, and some thought that HE was a demon, or a fraud, who, went about deceiving the people. However, because the Jewish leaders had the power to cut any Jewish person off from Israel's religious and social life, no one dared say anything favorably about JESUS in public (Vs.10-13).

Suddenly, midway through the festival, to everyone's surprise, JESUS boldly shows up in the temple, and begins to teach. The Jewish leaders, who had made themselves responsible for any advanced theological training, were amazed at JESUS' deep knowledge of scriptures. They couldn't even imagine how it was possible for JESUS to have acquired such knowledge without any of their help and training.

JESUS, however, explains to them that HE was not teaching HIS OWN ideas the way they were, but rather, HE was teaching the ideology of the GOD WHO sent HIM. HE further explained, that, anyone wanting to do the will of GOD would recognize the truth in HIS teachings, and that, HIS teachings are truly from GOD. In fact, HE said, those who teach their own ideas are seeking only to win praise for themselves and are not really interested in honoring GOD at all. JESUS goes on to tell them, that, in truth, they were not only uninterested in honoring GOD, but they were actually plotting to kill HIM, WHOM GOD had sent to save the world (Vs.14-19).

JESUS then shows them one of the flaws in their own religious reasoning by using the example of the religious custom of "circumcision", which is performed on all Jewish males after they become eight days old. JESUS reminded them of the times when HE came under attack for working on the Sabbath, whenever HE would heal people on that sacred day. However, if the eighth day of a boy's life fell on the Sabbath, they would indeed, circumcise him anyway, making themselves hypocrites (Vs.20-24).

Many of the people were pretty impressed with JESUS' bold stand against the religious leaders, despite the fact that they were trying to kill HIM. They were beginning to wonder out loud that maybe the Pharisees knew themselves, that JESUS was indeed the MESSIAH HE claimed to be, and why else, would HE have the nerve to speak this boldly.

However, they were still confused because they had known JESUS and HIS whole family virtually all of HIS life, and they reasoned this fact among themselves (Vs.25-27). JESUS tells them that, even though they have known HIM all of HIS life in the physical earthly sense, they still didn't know the ONE HE came to represent, which is HIS FATHER GOD in Heaven. At that point the Jewish leaders tried to arrest HIM, but the hand of GOD protected HIM and wouldn't allow it, because HIS time of crucifixion had not yet come (Vs. 28-30).

Many began to make favorable comments, speaking out audibly about JESUS indeed being the promised MESSIAH. When the Pharisees heard these murmurings they again sent temple guards to arrest JESUS, and JESUS said to them that HE would be there just a little while longer. In other words, JESUS seemed to be telling them to come back later and I'll let you arrest ME as part of MY FATHER's plan, not the Pharisees plans. JESUS told them that HE would soon return to HIS FATHER, where they would not be able to find HIM, nor come to HIM. And the Jewish leaders were greatly puzzled by HIS saying (Vs. 31-36).

THE LAST DAY OF THE FEAST
(John 7:37-53)

7 **(37)** In the last day, that great day of the feast, JESUS stood and cried, saying, "If any man thirst, let him come unto ME, and drink. **(38)** He that believeth on ME, as the scripture hath said, out of HIS belly shall flow rivers of living water." **(39)** (But this spake HE of the SPIRIT, which they that believe on HIM should receive: for the HOLY GHOST was not yet given; because that JESUS was not yet glorified.) **(40)** Many of the people therefore, when they heard this saying, said, "Of a truth this is the prophet". **(41)** Others said, "This is the CHRIST. But some said, "Shall CHRIST come out of Galilee?" **(42)** Hath not the scripture said, "That CHRIST cometh of the seed of David, and out of the town of Bethlehem, where David was?" **(43)** So there was a division among the people because of HIM. **(44)** And some of them would have taken HIM; but no man laid hands on HIM. **(45)** Then came the officers to the chief priests and Pharisees; and they said unto them, "Why have ye not brought HIM?" **(46)** The officers answered, "Never man spake like this man." **(47)** Then answered them the Pharisees, "Are ye also deceived?" **(48)** Have any of the rulers or of the Pharisees believed HIM? **(49)** But this people who knoweth not the law are cursed." **(50)** Nicodemus saith unto them, "(He that came to JESUS by night, being one of them,) **(51)** "Doth our law judge any man, before it hear HIM, and know what he doeth?" **(52)** They answered and said unto him, "Art thou also of Galilee? Search and and look: for out of Galilee ariseth no prophet." **(53)** And every man went unto his own house.

COMMENTARY:

During the Feast of the Tabernacles, the Jews performed a daily procession ritual, whereby a priest would walk from the temple to the nearby Gihon Spring, and fill a gold pitcher with water. They would then walk back to the temple and pour the water out on the altar. All during the procession, a choir would sing the words of Isaiah 12:3, which states, "Therefore with joy shall ye draw water out of the wells of salvation" (KJV).

This ritual was in remembrance of GOD allowing Moses and Aaron to draw water from a rock as they and the Israelites had been wandering thirstily in the desert wilderness of Zin, at Kadesh (Numbers 20:8-11). It also spoke prophetically of the days of the Messiah, which was much to their own unawares, already at hand.

The final day of the feast was the most celebrated of the seven-day event, and JESUS used this climatic forum to maximize the effect of HIS message. HE stood up and shouted to the crowd, "If any man thirst let him come unto ME, and drink. He that believeth on ME, as the scripture has said, out of his belly shall flow rivers of living water".

These words of JESUS were uttered as a direct offer of salvation to the people of Jerusalem, however, HE was referring to spiritual baptizing, sealing, and the indwelling function of the HOLY SPIRIT, in this, "The Church Age", which officially began, on the day of the "Pentecost" (50 days after JESUS' ascension back into Heaven) (Acts 1:5-8). However, despite this offer, just like many today, the people remained divided in their belief and acceptance of this wonderful gift. They continued to debate JESUS' identity, as some believed HE was the MESIAH, and others wrestled with their logic, and questioned what they thought they knew of JESUS' ancestry. And though some wanted HIM arrested, none were bold enough to lay hands on HIM. Even the temple guards, who had been sent to arrest HIM, instead, returned to temple empty-handed. When asked by the leading priests and Pharisees why JESUS had not been arrested, they replied, "No one ever spoke the way this man does".

WHAT DID WE LEARN FROM CHAPTER SEVEN?
Here are some key points to remember

(1). JESUS' brothers did not believe that HE was the MESSIAH at this point (John 7:5). In fact, it was not until after JESUS' resurrection, that they finally believed.

(2). Midway through the festival, JESUS went up into the temple to preach, despite the threats of death that came from the Jewish leaders. (John 7:14)

(3). JESUS was not trained in, nor by, the institutions of men. (John 7:15)

(4). JESUS showed the religious leaders the hypocrisy of their ways. (John 7:21-24)

(5). On the last day of the festival, JESUS announced the coming of the HOLY SPIRIT, WHO would dwell in those who believe in HIM. (John 7:37-39)

(6). JESUS' announcement of the promise of LIVING WATER caused division in the hearts of the people. GOD's word will always work to separate the wheat from the tares, or in other words, the true believer from the unbeliever. (John 7:40-49)

(7). Nicodemus, who had spoken with JESUS earlier (John 3:1-21), speaks up in favor of treating JESUS fairly. (John 7:50-51)

CHAPTER EIGHT:

(48)

A WOMAN CAUGHT IN ADULTERY

SCRIPTURE:
The King James Version
(John 8:1-11)

8 **(1)** JESUS went unto the Mount of Olives. **(2)** And early in the morning HE came again into the temple, and all the people came unto HIM; and HE sat down, and taught them. **(3)** And the scribes and Pharisees brought unto HIM a woman taken in adultery; and when they had set her in the midst, **(4)** They say unto HIM, "MASTER, this woman was taken in adultery, in the very act, **(5)** Now Moses in the law commanded us, that such should be stoned: but what sayest THOU?" **(6)** This they said, tempting HIM, that they might have to accuse HIM. But JESUS stooped down, and with HIS finger wrote on the ground, as though HE heard them not. **(7)** So when they continued asking HIM, HE lifted up HIMSELF, and said unto them, "He that is without sin among you, let him first cast a stone at her". **(8)** And again HE stooped down, and wrote on the ground. **(9)** And they which heard it, being convicted by their own conscience, went out one by one, beginning at the eldest, even unto the last: and JESUS was left alone, and the woman standing in the midst. **(10)** When JESUS had lifted up HIMSELF, and saw none but the woman, HE said unto her, "Woman, are those thine accusers? Hath no man condemned thee?" **(11)** She said, "No man, LORD." And JESUS said unto her, "Neither do I condemn thee: go, and sin no more."

COMMENTARY:

The earliest and most reliable Greek manuscripts do not contain the passage found in John 7:53-8:11. Almost all textual scholars agree that these verses were not in the original manuscript of the Gospel of John. Even the style and vocabulary of this passage is clearly different from the rest of this Gospel. It was probably part of true oral tradition that was added to later Greek manuscripts by "Copyists", and even in those manuscripts, it is not always found in the same place as it is in our modern-day bibles.

In this passage, JESUS finds HIMSELF once again in conflict with the Jewish religious Hierarchy. This time, however, they are trying to set a trap, hoping to get enough evidence to arrest HIM at some future date. As usual, their plot falls to JESUS' divine wisdom.

Taking up at verse one, we see where JESUS has just returned from the Mount of Olives one morning, and gone into the temple. As soon as HE got there, a crowd gathered, and HE sat down to teach them. While HE was teaching, a group of teachers of religious law, and Pharisees, brought to HIM, a woman who had been caught in the act of adultery. Nothing is mentioned of the man who must have been with her, for they only seized the woman apparently.

But, anyway, there they stood with the woman while trying to trap JESUS with this question. "The law of Moses says that we should stone this woman to death for her sin of adultery, but what do YOU say?" JESUS stooped down and wrote in the dust with HIS finger, and after they continued to press HIM for an answer, HE said, "Ok go ahead and stone her, but let the one who is among you that has never sinned, throw the first stone." Then JESUS stooped down again and wrote in the dust with HIS finger. When the lady's accusers heard this, one by one, they slipped away, starting with the eldest, until all had gone from the lady's presence except JESUS.

All human beings have sinned and fallen short of the glory of JESUS. We cannot judge others for their sin, because we ourselves are, all, people under judgment. Only JESUS could judge that sinful woman that day in Jerusalem, and even HE chose not to do so, at that time. HE chose instead to forgive her and then send her on her way with the simple admonishment, that, she "sin no more".

That's what JESUS' vicarious sacrifice does for each of us. It redeems us and re-establishes us into a right relationship of friendship with GOD, and, it also frees us from the punishment of death, because we have proven ourselves, long ago, of being incapable of following the letter of the law.

JESUS IS THE LIGHT OF THE WORLD
John 8:12-20

8 (12) Then JESUS spake again unto them, saying, "I AM the light of the world: he that followeth ME shall not walk in darkness, but shall have the light of life." (13) The Pharisees therefore said unto HIM, "THOU bearest record of THYSELF; THY record is not true." (14) JESUS answered and said unto them, "Though I bear record of MYSELF, yet MY record is true: for I know whence I came, and whither I go; but ye cannot tell whence I come, and whither I go. (15) Ye judge after the flesh; I judge no man. (16) And yet if I judge, MY judgment is true: for I AM not alone, but I and the FATHER that sent ME. (17) It is also written in your law, that the testimony of two men is true. (18) I AM ONE that bears witness of

MYSELF, and the FATHER that sent ME beareth witness of ME." (19) Then said they unto HIM, "Where is THY FATHER? JESUS answered, "Ye neither know ME, nor MY FATHER: if ye had known ME, ye should have known MY FATHER also." (20) These words spake JESUS in the treasury, as HE taught in the temple: and no man laid hands on HIM; for HIS hour was not yet come.

COMMENTARY:

In the New Testament Greek, the word most often used for "light" is "phos" (foce), and it means "to make shine, or manifest in the widest application". In the Gospel of John, the word "light" is closely associated with distinguishing between that which is true, and that which is false.

As the "LIGHT OF THE WORLD", JESUS becomes the only source of illumination of spiritual reality that this world will ever know. To believe in HIM, is to see all things as they really are. To not believe in HIM, is to be left with only our own human standards and ingenuity, and, of course, darkness.

In John 8:12, JESUS gives us the second of HIS seven great "I AM Statements". "I AM the light of the world" is what HE said to a packed house in the "Women's Court" of the Temple at Jerusalem, during the "Torch Lighting" ceremonies of the Feast of the Tabernacles.

One of the major features of the feast was the lighting of giant torches whose wicks were made from some of the worn out garments of the priests. The torches illuminated the court area and the people sang praises to GOD and danced. The torch lighting was in commemoration of how GOD was with the Israelites in a pillar of clouds by day, and, in a pillar of fire by night, as they wandered in the desert after being released from bondage in Egypt (Numbers 9:15-23).

How fitting it was for JESUS to make this grand statement at this particular time, while the large torches were burning, and everyone's minds were focused on the annual bright lighting of the Temple in Jerusalem. In the Bible, light is a symbol of THE ALMIGHTY GOD and HIS Holiness. Here JESUS is plainly stating that HE is not just "a light", or even, merely "another light among many", but HE is "THE LIGHT" for the whole world. He, who is wise enough to choose to follow JESUS, will never again walk in darkness. That doesn't mean that he will never sin again, it only means he will never be able to live comfortably in his sin. He will not remain under the dominion of sin and darkness, because he has THE CHRIST to light his way.

JESUS never really answered the religious leaders' question of "Where is YOUR FATHER?" Still HE didn't really avoid it either, but rather, HE addressed it honestly. JESUS fully knew that their father was certainly not GOD. In fact, HE even knew that their father was satan. Yes, even though they were religious leaders in Jerusalem, they were still children of the devil. This was, of course, evidenced in their continued attempts, to arrest JESUS. They had been unsuccessful in doing so, up until this point, because JESUS' hour of passion had not yet come.

A WARNING TO THE UNBELIEVERS
John 8:21-30

8 (21) Then said JESUS again unto them, "I go MY way, and ye shall seek ME, and shall die in your sins: whither I go, ye cannot come." (22) Then said the Jews, "Will HE kill HIMSELF? Because HE saith, "Whither I go, ye cannot come. (23) And HE said unto them, "Ye are from beneath; I AM from above: ye are of this world; I AM not of this world. (24) I said therefore unto you, that ye shall die in your sins: for if ye believe not that I AM HE, ye shall die in your sins" (25) Then said they unto HIM, "WHO art THOU?" And JESUS saith unto them, "Even the same that I said unto you from the beginning. (26) I have many things to say and to judge of you: but HE that sent ME is true; and I speak to the world those things which I have heard of HIM." (27) They understood not that HE spake to them of the FATHER. (28) Then said JESUS unto them, "When ye have lifted up the SON of man, then shall ye know that I AM HE, and that I do nothing of MYSELF; but as MY FATHER hath taught ME, I speak these things. (29) And HE that sent ME is with ME: the FATHER hath not left ME alone; for I do always those things that please HIM." (30) As HE spake these words, many believed on HIM.

COMMENTARY:

The true Christian dies in the LORD because he lives in the LORD. By contrast, the unbeliever dies in his sin because he lives in his sin. The sin of man is his unbelief in CHRIST JESUS. In John 8:21-30, JESUS issues another stern warning to those who refused to believe on HIM before it is too late. And just as JESUS' time left on this earth was very short at that point, so were their opportunities to get to know HIM, also very limited. They were squandering away the opportunities GOD had given them, by arguing with JESUS, instead of learning to trust in HIM.

In this passage, once again JESUS speaks about soon going away to a place where they could not follow HIM. The puzzled Jewish leaders thought that he was speaking of committing suicide, which was a detestable thing in the Jewish community. The Jews have always been taught to respect all of life. To commit suicide meant that a person would automatically go to a place of judgment, and being the righteous people that they thought they were, there would be no way that they could follow JESUS there. But in verses 23-24, JESUS tells them that they "are from below, or "of this earth" and I AM not. That is why I said that you will die in your sins. Unless you believe that I AM WHO I say I AM, you will indeed die in your sins." Incredibly, the Jews continued to ask WHO JESUS was, even though HE had given them all kinds of evidence as to HIM being the SON of the living GOD that they claimed they themselves worshiped.

The revelation of CHRIST JESUS as "I AM" in verse 25 only further confused these spiritual dimwits, and HIS words regarding their sins probably infuriated them also. JESUS could have said much more to HIS unbelieving audience, and certainly HE was more than qualified to condemn them. However the whole purpose of HIS first advent was to save the world, not condemn it.

Unfortunately, HIS message was one that they could not hear, because GOD was simply unknown to them. Their lack of spiritual understanding caused them to totally miss JESUS and HIS life-giving message of salvation. JESUS told them that only when they have lifted HIM up on the cross, would they fully realize WHO HE was. By this, HE did not mean that all of them would be saved, but rather, that the cross would reveal that HE was GOD's LIVING WORD delivered directly to man, in an effort to save him.

JESUS AND ABRAHAM
John 8:31-59

8 (31) Then JESUS said to those Jews which believed on HIM, "If ye continue in MY word, then are ye MY disciples indeed; (32) And ye shall know the truth, and the truth shall make you free." (33) They answered HIM, "We be Abraham's seed, and were never in bondage to any man: how sayest THOU, Ye shall be made free?" (34) JESUS answered them, "Verily, verily I say unto you, Whosoever committeth sin is the servant of sin. (35) And the servant abideth not in the house for ever: but the SON abideth ever. (36) If the SON therefore shall make you free, ye shall be free indeed. (37) I know that ye are Abraham's seed; but ye seek to kill ME, because MY word hath no place in you. (38) I speak that which I have seen with

MY FATHER: and ye do that which ye have seen with your father." (39) They answered and said unto HIM, "Abraham is our father. JESUS saith unto them, "If ye were Abraham's children, ye would do the works of Abraham. (40) But now ye seek to kill ME, a MAN that hath told you the truth, which I have heard of GOD: this did not Abraham. (41) Ye do the deeds of your father." Then said they to HIM, "We be not born of fornication; we have one father, even GOD. (42) JESUS said unto them, "If GOD were your FATHER, ye would love ME: for I proceeded forth and came from GOD; neither came I of MYSELF, but HE sent ME. (43) Why do ye not understand MY speech? Even because ye cannot hear MY word. (44) Ye are of your father the devil, and the lusts of your father ye will do. He was a murderer from the beginning, and abode not in the truth, because there is no truth in him. When he speaketh a lie, he speaketh of his own: for he is a liar, and the father of it. (45) And because I tell you the truth, ye believe ME not. (46) Which of you convinceth ME of sin? And if I say the truth, why do ye not believe ME? (47) He that is of GOD heareth GOD's words: ye therefore hear them not, because ye are not of GOD." (48) Then answered the Jews, and said unto HIM, "Say we not well that THOU art a Samaritan, and hast a devil? (49) JESUS answered, "I have not a devil; but I honour MY FATHER, and ye do dishonour ME. (50) And I seek not MINE OWN glory: there is ONE that seeketh and judgeth. (51) Verily, verily I say unto you, If a man keep MY saying, he shall never see death. (52) Then said the Jews unto HIM, "Now we know that THOU hast a devil. Abraham is dead, and the prophets; and THOU sayeest, "If a man keep MY saying, he shall never taste of death. (53) Art THOU greater than our father Abraham, which is dead? And the prophets are dead: whom makest THOU THYSELF? (54) JESUS answered, "If I honour MYSELF, MY honour is nothing: it is MY FATHER that honoureth ME; of WHOM ye say, that HE is your GOD: (55) Yet ye have not known HIM; but I know HIM: and if I should say, I know HIM not, I shall be a liar like unto you: but I know HIM, and keep HIS saying. (56) Your father Abraham rejoiced to see MY day: and he saw it , and was glad." (57) The said the Jews unto HIM, "THOU art not yet fifty years old, and hast THOU seen Abraham?" (58) JESUS said unto them, "Verily, verily I say unto you, Before Abraham was, I AM." (59) Then took they up stones to cast at HIM: but JESUS hid HIMSELF, and went out of the temple, going through the midst of them, and so passed by.

COMMENTARY:

A closed mind puts an end to discipleship before it begins. One must have an open mind before they can believe, and they must be receptive, before they can receive, and then finally, they must be willing to obey, that which they do perceive. In other words, true disciples learn, in order that they may do that which they have learned.

In the Gospel according to the Apostle John, in chapter 8, verses 31-32 (KJV), JESUS tells a group of believers, who gathered around HIM in the Temple at Jerusalem that, "If ye continue in MY Word, then are ye MY disciples indeed; And ye shall know the truth, and the truth shall set you free".

They responded by saying that they were the descendants of Abraham, and were never in bondage to any man. Ironically, even as they spoke, they were being oppressed by the Romans, who ruled over most of the known world at that time. Not to mention their previous history of bondage in Egypt, Syria, and Babylon, how soon the human mind forgets.

Probably, in the biblical sense, there are basically two kinds of Prophets. The one who delivers a message of how we can be spiritually free, and the one, who delivers a message to those, who think they are free, but are in fact, in spiritual bondage. Here in this passage, John 8:34-59, we see JESUS taking on the role of the latter.

Throughout this passage, we see CHRIST trying to deliver a spiritual message to a group of religious leaders, who surprisingly, only seem to be able to listen physically, and can't seem to find a place in their hearts to receive HIS words spiritually.

In verses 34-35, JESUS tells them that everyone who sins is a slave to sin, and that a slave is not a permanent member of the family. Remember, in Abraham's family, he fathered Ishmael by the Egyptian servant-girl, Hagar, outside of the will of GOD and they were later, cast out of the house, by Abraham, even though Ishmael was his descendant (Genesis 21:8-21). Isaac was the son who belonged and therefore, he remained in the house.

And so, we see, that, though both sons were descendants of Abraham, one belonged spiritually (within the will of GOD), and the other didn't. JESUS goes on to tell them that if they were children of Abraham, they would follow Abraham's example of faith and belief in FATHER GOD, and they wouldn't be trying to kill HIM. The angry religious leaders then shouted, "We are not born out of wedlock! Our true father is GOD HIMSELF! JESUS then replies, "If GOD were your father, you would love ME, because I have come from HIM".

The confused religious leaders continued to press their point and JESUS bluntly warned them of being in danger of dying in their own sins, unless they begin to believe in HIM. It is foolish to rely on a physical descent from Abraham, or anyone else, when only spiritual kinship to CHRIST JESUS is our ticket out of the bondage of our sins. Antagonism toward JESUS, only proves that we are in the spiritual lineage of satan, and are unrelated to GOD.

"YAHWEH", in the Hebrew language, is the personal name for GOD in the Old Testament, and it is translated in the English, "I AM". In John 8:58, JESUS tells the crowd who gathered before HIM, that, "Verily, verily, I say unto you, "Before Abraham was, I AM". In saying that, the crowd knew what HE was insinuating, and begin picking up stones to try and kill HIM. They believed that HE had blasphemed, by calling HIMSELF GOD. By saying that HE saw Abraham, and, in affirming the eternity of HIS OWN being, JESUS, that day, laid claim to being the GOD of the Old Testament, and the Jews were clearly infuriated, by the truth of HIS words.

True freedom can only come by knowing CHRIST JESUS, and we must come to recognize the difference between "freedom" and "liberty". "Liberty" is "the free will of choice", that GOD has given to each of us, and "freedom" can only be realized, when and if, we use that liberty to choose the SON, that FATHER GOD HIMSELF has already sent into world.

WHAT DID WE LEARN FROM CHAPTER EIGHT?
Here are some key points to remember

(1). One man cannot judge another man for his sins, because, all mankind has sinned, and, as a result, are all under judgment themselves, from GOD. (John 8:1-11)

(2). JESUS represents the "light", or "way out of sin and darkness" for all mankind. (John 8:12-20)

(3). We must believe in CHRIST in order to receive salvation. (John 8:21-30)

(4). JESUS' "first coming" was to save, not to judge. (John 8:26)

(5). Only CHRIST JESUS can truly set us free. (John 8:31-36)

(6). True Christians listen to and try to obey the word of GOD. (John 8:47)

(7). JESUS existed before Abraham was born. (John 8:58)

CHAPTER NINE:

JESUS HEALS A MAN BORN BLIND

SCRIPTURE:
The King James Version
John 9:1-34

9 **(1)** And as JESUS passed by, HE saw a man which was blind from his birth. **(2)** And HIS disciples asked HIM, saying, "MASTER, who did sin, this man, or his parents, that he was born blind?" **(3)** JESUS answered, "Neither hath this man sinned, nor his parents: but that the work of GOD should be made manifest in him. **(4)** I must work the works of HIM that sent ME, while it is day: the night cometh, when no man can work. **(5)** As long as I AM in the world, I AM the light of the world." **(6)** When HE had thus spoken, HE spat on the ground, and made clay of the spittle, and HE anointed the eyes of the blind man with the clay, **(7)** And said unto him, "Go, wash in the pool of Siloam", (which is by interpretation, "Sent".) He went his way therefore, and washed, and came seeing. **(8)** The neighbors therefore, and they which before had seen him that he was blind, said, "Is not this he that sat and begged?" **(9)** Some said, "He is like him: but he said, I am he". **(10)** Therefore they said unto him, "How were thine eyes opened?" **(11)** He answered and said, "A MAN that is called JESUS made clay, and anointed mine eyes, and said, "Go to the pool of Siloam, and wash: and I went and washed, and I received sight." **(12)** Then said they unto him, "Where is HE?" He said, "I know not." **(13)** They brought to the Pharisees him that aforetime was blind. **(14)** And it was the Sabbath day when JESUS made the clay, and opened his eyes. **(15)** Then again the Pharisees also asked him how he had received his sight. He said unto them, "HE put clay upon mine eyes, and I washed, and do see." **(16)** Therefore said some of the Pharisees, "This MAN is not of GOD, because HE keepeth not the Sabbath day. Others said, "How can a man that is a sinner do such miracles?" And there was a division among them. **(17)** They say unto the blind man again, "What sayest thou of HIM, that HE hath opened thine eyes?" He said, "HE is a prophet."
(18) But the Jews did not believe concerning him, that he had been blind, and received his sight, until they called the parents of him that had received his sight. **(19)** And they asked them, saying, "Is this your son, who ye say was born blind? How then doth he now see?" **(20)** His parents answered them and said, "We know that this is our son, and that he was born blind: **(21)** But by what means he now seeth, we know not; or WHO hath opened his eyes, we know not: he is of age; ask him: he shall speak for himself."

(22) These words spake his parents, because they feared the Jews: for the Jews had agreed already, that if any man did confess that HE was CHRIST, he should be put out of the synagogue. (23) Therefore said his parents, "He is of age; ask him." (24) Then again called they the man that was blind, and said unto him, "Give GOD the praise: we know that this MAN is a sinner." (25) He answered and said, "Whether HE be a sinner or no, I know not: one thing I know, that, whereas I was blind, now I see." (26) Then said they to him again, "What did HE to thee? How opened HE thine eyes?" (27) He answered them, "I have told you already, and ye did not hear: wherefore would ye hear it again? Will ye also be HIS disciples?" (28) Then they reviled him, and said, "Thou art HIS disciple; but we are Moses' disciples. (29) We know that GOD spake unto Moses: as for this FELLOW, we know not from whence HE is." (30) The man answered and said unto them, "Why herein is a marvelous thing, that ye know not from whence HE is, and yet HE has opened mine eyes. (31) Now we know that GOD heareth not sinners: but if any man be a worshipper of GOD, and doeth HIS will, him HE heareth. (32) Since the world began was it not heard that any man opened the eyes of one that was born blind. (33) If this MAN were not of GOD, HE could do nothing." (34) They answered and said unto him, "Thou wast altogether born in sins, and dost thou teach us?" And they cast him out.

COMMENTARY:

In John chapter nine, opposition to JESUS continues to intensify, as we see that the popular Old Testament time's theology, that accredited a person's sickness or death as punishment for their sins, was still a prevalent belief among the Jewish people of Jerusalem in the first century.

As JESUS was walking along the streets of Jerusalem one day, HE encountered a man who had been blind from birth. His disciples asked HIM why the man had been born blind. Was it because, of his own sins, or, was it because of the sins of his parents? JESUS answers that it is neither, but rather, he was born blind so that the power of GOD could be manifest in him.

Even though sickness and sin can be related, in that, the fall of man, through Adam, introduced both into the world, individual death and suffering, that we experience, are not necessarily a punishment for our individual sins. However, death and sickness can both be viewed as a witness to the continuing sinful condition, or state, of humanity.

Here in this passage, the disciples weren't moved by compassion for the blind man, but rather, they were moved by theological curiosity, and the cause of his condition. Like CHRIST, our first concern must be for the person who is suffering, and how we can meet their needs. We can focus later on, on how they got were they are, and, how we can help them to avoid going astray again.

All of us have tasks that have been assigned to us by GOD and whether we realize it or not, we only have a short time to perform those duties here on earth. While we are still in the world, like CHRIST, we must strive to be "a light in the world" for others to see (Vs. 4-5). The unique thing about JESUS' healing of the blind man, here in this passage, is that, JESUS did not even promise healing. Here HE simply smears the mud from HIS spit on the eyes of the man and instructs him on what to do after that. But because the man was obedient to the word of CHRIST, he was able to gain his sight for the very first time. It is an illustration of what JESUS had already expressed to HIS disciples earlier in John 8:31-32, where HE stated that, "You are truly MY disciples if you continue to obey MY teachings, and you will know the truth, and the truth will set you free".

When we put JESUS' words into action, we inevitably come to know the truth. We can then, both, see the spiritual reality, and, we can also experience its goodness. After being cured, this man had a hard time persuading the people and the Pharisees that his healing by JESUS was real. However, the man boldly proclaimed that the miracle on his eyes could only have been accomplished by a man who actually came from GOD, and not from some sinner, like the Pharisees tried to lead people to believe JESUS was.

Even today, JESUS is still doing those things that are considered by the unbeliever to be too good to be true, and the Pharisees like many today, were always trying to condemn anyone whose idea of religion was not their own. In fact, that is why we have so many different denominations and sects available to us today. It seems that everyone wants a GOD that they can create in their own image, or a GOD that fits their lifestyle in the most comfortable way.

The Pharisees were comfortable with being, what they called, "Disciples of Moses". They felt that they knew who Moses was, but unfortunately, they knew nothing of JESUS (V. 29). The man replied how strange it is that JESUS had healed his eyes, and they, who were of the religious hierarchy in Jerusalem, didn't even know anything about HIM. And even though no one in the history of the world, at that time, had ever restored sight to a person that had been born blind, the Pharisees still couldn't bring themselves to accept that JESUS was truly sent by GOD. As a result of his bold testimony about his belief in CHRIST JESUS, the once, "blind man" was promptly thrown out of the synagogue, by the hard-hearted, angry Pharisees.

The blind man in this biblical account was bolder than his parents, who had refused to take a stand on the fact that their son had been obviously miraculously healed by JESUS. The parent's position on this matter was heavily influenced by the known hostilities of the religious leaders towards JESUS, and anyone who sided with HIM. However, as far as the son was concerned, the blessing of restored sight was too great to ignore, and he was determined not to be intimidated by the Jewish religious leaders.

We can all learn a lesson from the son in this story, on how we ourselves need to share our own faith in CHRIST, because there is nothing that we can possibly lose that would compare to what we have gained by knowing CHRIST JESUS as our LORD and SAVIOR.

SPIRITUAL BLINDNESS
John 9:35-41

9 (35) JESUS heard that they had cast him out; and when HE had found him, HE said unto him, "Dost thou believe on the SON of GOD?" (36) He answered and said, "WHO is HE, LORD, that I might believe on HIM? (37) And JESUS said unto him, "Thou hast both seen HIM, and it is HE that talketh with thee."

(38) And he said, "LORD, I believe". And he worshipped HIM. (39) And JESUS said, "For judgment I AM come into this world, that they which see not might see; and that they which see might be made blind." (40) And some of the Pharisees which were with him heard these words, and said unto HIM, "Are we blind also?" (41) JESUS said unto them, "If ye were blind, ye should have no sin: but now ye say, "We see"; therefore your sin remaineth."

COMMENTARY:

After JESUS heard that the man whom HE had cured of a life-long blindness had been excommunicated from the temple at Jerusalem, HE went looking for him, just as any good shepherd would do. When HE found him HE asked him if he believed in the SON of MAN. The man responded by asking JESUS, WHO the SON of MAN was. Remember, when the man first met JESUS he could not see HIM, and could only hear HIS voice. He would not be able to recognized JESUS by sight at this point. And so JESUS says to the man, "It is HE, WHO is speaking to you right now." And the man, immediately believed, and begin to worship JESUS in the presence of a few of the Pharisees, who were standing there.

JESUS then says to the man, "I have come into the world to judge the world, to give sight to the blind, and to show those who think they see, that they are blind." The observing Pharisees were disturbed at what JESUS said, and must have also certainly been vexed by JESUS' acceptance of worship from the man whom they had ostracized from the temple just moments earlier. They contemptuously state to JESUS, "Are YOU calling us blind?" JESUS tells them, "If you were blind, you wouldn't be guilty, but you remain guilty, because you claim you can see".

Here JESUS is speaking of the Pharisees' spiritual blindness. It was a blindness caused by pride, self-righteousness, their tradition, and their inability to properly interpret the Word of GOD. HE was telling them that they would be much better off, if they were physically blind, than they were at that point. Because, if they were physically blind, they would have an excuse for not knowing what was going on. However, since they claimed that they understood GOD's Word, they made themselves guilty, not only by denying themselves the Word of GOD, but also, by denying the Jewish people, the truth, of those words.

WHAT DID WE LEARN FROM CHAPTER NINE?
Here are some key points to remember

(1). The healing of the blind man was the sixth sign of the Messiah.

(2). Death and suffering are not necessarily punishment for our individual sin, however, they may be a witness to our sinful condition, or, even a way for GOD to express or manifest HIS power, through us. (John 9:1-4)

(3). Like CHRIST, our first concern should be for the sufferer, not the cause of his suffering. That issue can many times be addressed after you've given the sufferer some relief . (John 9:1-7)

(4). Witness is simply telling what you know by experience. You don't have to know much about JESUS, before you're able to tell someone what HE has done for you. (John 9:9-33)

(5). Your witness of JESUS will sometimes offend people and cause them to separate themselves from you. (John 9:34)

(6). Quickly use every opportunity GOD gives you to witness of CHRIST and help someone else in their time of need. (John 9:4)

(7). The Pharisees' rejection of CHRIST was deliberate, and thereby, they were guilty of the worst kind of sin a person can commit. (John 9:40-41)

CHAPTER TEN:

THE GOOD SHEPHERD: LISTENING WITH DISCERNMENT

SCRIPTURE:
The King James Version
John 10:1-21

10 (1) "Verily, verily, I say unto you, He that entereth not by the door into the sheepfold, but climbeth up some other way, the same is a thief and a robber. **(2)** But he that entereth in by the door is the shepherd of the sheep. **(3)** To him the porter openeth; and the sheep hear his voice: and he calleth his own sheep by name, and leadeth them out. **(4)** And when he putteth forth his own sheep, he goeth before them, and the sheep follow him: for they know his voice. **(5)** And a stranger will they not follow, but will flee from him: for they know not the voice of strangers." **(6)** This parable spake JESUS unto them: but they understood not what things they were which HE spake unto them. **(7)** Then said JESUS unto them again, "Verily, verily, I say unto you, I AM the door of the sheep. **(8)** All that ever came before ME are thieves and robbers: but the sheep did not hear them. **(9)** I AM the DOOR: by ME if any man enter in, he shall be saved, and shall go in and out, and find pasture. **(10)** The thief cometh not, but for to steal, and to kill, and to destroy: I AM come that they might have life, and that they might have it more abundantly. **(11)** I AM the GOOD SHEPHERD: the GOOD SHEPHERD giveth HIS life for the sheep. **(12)** But he that is an hireling, and not the shepherd, whose own the sheep are not, seeth the wolf coming, and leaveth the sheep, and fleeth: and the wolf catcheth them, and scattereth the sheep. **(13)** The hireling fleeth, because he is an hireling, and careth not for the sheep. **(14)** I AM the GOOD SHEPHERD, and know MY sheep, and am known of MINE. **(15)** As the FATHER knoweth ME, even so I know the FATHER: and I lay down MY life for the sheep. **(16)** And other sheep I have, which are not of this fold: them also I must bring, and they shall hear MY voice; and there shall be one fold, and one shepherd. **(17)** Therefore doth MY FATHER love ME, because I lay down MY life, that I might take it up again. **(18)** No man taketh it from ME, but I lay it down of MYSELF. I have power to lay it down, and I have power to take it up again. This commandment have I received of MY FATHER." **(19)** There was a division therefore again among the Jews for these sayings. **(20)** And many of them said, "HE hath a devil, and is mad; why hear ye HIM?" **(21)** Others said, "These are not the words of him that hath a devil. Can a devil open the eyes of the blind?"

COMMENTARY:

In the Greek, the word used for "thief" is "kleptes" (klep-tace), and it describes "one who takes by stealth or by covert means". By contrast, the Greek word used for "robber" is "lestes" (lace-tace), and it describes "one who takes by force". In John chapter 10, verse 1, the thief, that JESUS is alluding to, could be any of the Pharisees, the religious leaders of that day, who took by subtle and unsuspecting methods.

The robber, that JESUS makes mention of in this passage, can be likened to any of the Romans, who took, or stole from the Israelites by imposing their will, authority, and power upon them. It was those kinds of leaderships that JESUS sought to expose and put an end to forever, and it was certainly not the kind of leadership that HE intended for HIS new upcoming "Christian Church".

Perhaps there is no more endearing image of JESUS in all of Scripture, than the one HE presents of HIMSELF as the "Good Shepherd" in John chapter 10. The imagery of the Good Shepherd is forever woven in the minds and hearts of all who believe in CHRIST JESUS.

The Bible is rife with passages that use the analogy of the loving Shepherd as a provider and protector of that which he oversees. He is one who risks his life to seek and save, even that one straying sheep, who may have separated itself from his beloved flock.

The leaders of the Christian church can also be likened to the good Shepherd, and the members of their congregation, can be likened to the flock. It is the duty of the pastor to spiritually lead, and feed his flock with the nourishing food of the Word of GOD. He must, do so, willingly and eagerly, without constraints, not for the love of money, nor, for the power that he has obtained, due to his position. He must lead by example, and his behavior must paint a picture of the patience and love of GOD, our LORD and SAVIOR, through JESUS CHRIST.

In the Latin Vulgate, the word Jerome uses for "Pastor" is "Shepherd" in Ephesians 4:11. It describes the function of one in such a position in the church. It is the duty of each member of the flock, to come into a personal relationship with the SHEPHERD, because of their continued need for HIS love, guidance, and protection. They should always be able to discern HIS voice from all other voices, and also be able to distinguish that which is representative of HIS work.

The only way, to achieve that kind of relationship with GOD, is by familiarizing oneself with the SHEPHERD, JESUS CHRIST, WHO is "The Word". One can thereby, ultimately realize the purpose for which he has came into the fold (world), and that is, of course, to serve and obey GOD.

GOD's voice can only be heard, through a leader who has patterned his life after the examples of service that were shown to us by JESUS CHRIST during HIS three-year ministry. JESUS' impeccable standards will manifest themselves through anyone who represents HIS cause.

There is no way to mistaken HIS unique and lofty standards for those of any "false representatives" that may have came down the pike, either before, or since HIS time. One only needs to know JESUS the SHEPHERD, WHO is the real deal, in order to discern the fakes, who misrepresent, in the name of the LORD.

Just as every good shepherd knows his sheep, every good sheep should come to know his shepherd's voice. Such knowledge can mean the difference between life and death, in many cases. It can also be the difference between danger and safety, starvation and nourishment, or, shelter and homelessness.

To be alone in this world, and have no hope of anything beyond this world, is a frightening thought. We as Christians, no longer have to entertain, or envision that thought. And so, we should be forever thankful to our "GOOD SHEPHERD", our LORD and SAVIOR JESUS CHRIST, for making the wonderful gift of Eternal Life in GOD's own glorious presence, a reality, by way of HIS vicarious sacrifice on the cross at Golgotha.

JESUS' LAST PUBLIC TEACHING
John 10: 22-42

10 22) And it was at Jerusalem the feast of the dedication, and it was winter. **(23)** And JESUS walked in the temple in Solomon's porch. **(24)** Then came the Jews round about HIM, and said unto HIM, "How long dost THOU make us to doubt? If THOU be the CHRIST, tell us plainly. **(25)** JESUS answered them, "I told you, and ye believed not: the works that I do in MY FATHER's name, they bear witness of ME. **(26)** But ye believe not, because ye are not of MY sheep, as I said unto you. **(27)** MY sheep hear MY voice, and I know them, and they follow ME: **(28)** And I give unto them eternal life; and they shall never perish, neither shall any man pluck them out of MY FATHER's hand. **(29)** MY FATHER, which gave them ME, is greater than all; and no man is able to pluck them out of MY FATHER's hand. **(30)** I and MY FATHER are one." **(31)** Then the Jews took up stones again to stone HIM. **(32)** JESUS answered them, "Many good works have I shewed you from MY FATHER; for which of those works do ye stone ME?" **(33)** The Jews answered HIM, saying, "For a good work we stone THEE not; but for blasphemy; and because that THOU, being a man, makest THYSELF GOD." (34) JESUS answered them, "Is it not written in your law, "I said, ye are GODS? (35) If HE called them gods, unto whom the word of GOD came, and the scripture cannot be broken; (36) Say ye of HIM, WHOM the FATHER hath sanctified, and sent into the world, thou blasphemest; because I said, I AM the SON of GOD? (37) If I do not the works of MY FATHER, believe ME not. (38) But if I do, though you believe not ME, believe the works: that ye may know, and believe, that the FATHER is in ME, and I in HIM." (39) Therefore they sought again to take HIM: but HE escaped out of their hand, (40) And went away again beyond Jordan into the place where John at first baptized; and there HE abode. (41) And many resorted unto HIM, and said, "John did no miracle: but all things that John spake of this man were true. (42) And many believed on HIM there.

COMMENTARY:

In John 10:22-42, the apostle gives an account of the last public confrontation of JESUS with the hostile Jews at Jerusalem. It occurs during the Jewish festival of "Hanukkah", an eight-day feast, which is held in December, and commemorates the re-consecration of the temple by Judas Maccabeus in 165 B.C., after it had been desecrated by Antiochus IV Epiphanes in 168 B.C.

To the Jews, the feast was a reminder of their last great victory over their enemies, the Assyrians. During the "Macabean Revolt", led by Judas Macabeus, the Jews recaptured the city of Jerusalem and held it until the great Roman general Pompey recaptured it and brought it under Roman control in 63 B.C., successfully ending the 100-plus year reign of the Hasmonean Dynasty of the Macabees family.

Here in this passage, as JESUS was walking through the section of the temple, known as Solomon's Porch one day, HE was approached and surrounded by a group of Jewish religious leaders, who demanded for HIM to plainly tell them if HE was the MESSIAH or not. Apparently JESUS' enigmatic sayings had troubled them greatly in the two months since they had last encountered HIM at the Feast of the Tabernacles.

JESUS' reply to the insistent group was that HE had already told them, and also shown them through HIS miracles, and, despite what he had told and shown them, they still didn't believe HIM, because they were not a part of HIS flock. HE then tells them that, if they were a part of HIS flock they would understand HIM, and follow HIM, and no one would be able to pull them away from HIM. Eternal life would be theirs simply because, they believe on HIM, and, because HE and the FATHER are one.

Angered by JESUS' comments, the Jewish leaders picked up stones and readied themselves to kill HIM. JESUS asked them, "For which good deed are you stoning ME? The Jews replied that they were going to stone HIM, because HE claimed to be GOD. When JESUS said that HE and the FATHER are one, HE was not affirming that HE and GOD was the same person, but rather, HE was saying that HE and GOD have the closest possible unity of purpose.

After a few more minutes of debate, JESUS whisked HIMSELF away from the angry crowd and went across the Jordan River and dwelled near the place where John the Baptist had once baptized. And many followed HIM and came to believe on HIM in that place.

WHAT DID WE LEARN FROM CHAPTER TEN?
Here are some key points to remember

(1). In JESUS' parable of the Good Shepherd, the "thief" represents the Pharisees, because they took from the Jews by stealth and subtle methods.

(2). In JESUS' parable of the Good Shepherd, the "robber" represents the Roman authorities, who, took from the Jews by force.

(3). JESUS is the DOOR than opens into Salvation and Heaven. (John 10:6 & 9)

(4). JESUS is the GOOD SHEPHERD, WHO was willing to lay down HIS life for us, HIS sheep.

(5). JESUS knows the heart of HIS followers, just as GOD the FATHER knows HIS heart. John 10:14-15)

(6). JESUS gives eternal life to all who accept and follow HIM. (John 10:27-28)

(7). Once you give your life to CHRIST, no one can take you away from HIM. HE and FATHER GOD are of one purpose. (John 10:29-30)

CHAPTER ELEVEN:

(67)

THE PHYSICAL DEATH AND RESURRECTION OF LAZARUS

SCRIPTURE:
The King James Version
(John 11:1-44)

11 **(1)** Now a certain man was sick, named Lazarus, of Bethany, the town of Mary and her sister Martha. **(2)** (It was that Mary which anointed the LORD with ointment, and wiped HIS feet with her hair, whose brother Lazarus was sick.) **(3)** Therefore his sisters sent unto HIM, saying, LORD, behold, he whom THOU lovest is sick. **(4)** When JESUS heard that, HE said, "This sickness is not unto death, but for the glory of GOD, that the SON of GOD might be glorified thereby." **(5)** Now JESUS loved Martha, and her sister, and Lazarus. **(6)** When HE had heard therefore that he was sick, HE abode two days still in the same place where HE was. **(7)** Then after that saith HE to HIS disciples, "Let us go unto Judaea again." **(8)** HIS disciples say unto HIM, "MASTER, the Jews of late sought to stone THEE; and goeth THOU thither again? **(9)** JESUS answered, "Are there not twelve hours in the day? If any man walk in the day, he stumbleth not, because he seeth the light of this world. **(10)** But if a man walk in the night, he stumbleth, because there is no light in him." **(11)** These things said HE: and after that HE saith unto them, "Our friend Lazarus sleepeth; but I go, that I may awake him out of sleep." **(12)** Then said HIS disciples, "LORD, if he sleep, he shall do well. **(13)** Howbeit JESUS spake of his death: but they thought that HE had spoken of taking of rest in sleep. **(14)** Then said JESUS unto them plainly, "Lazarus is dead. **(15)** And I AM glad for your sakes that I was not there, to the intent ye may believe; nevertheless let us go unto him." **(16)** Then said Thomas, which is called Didymus, unto his fellow disciples, "Let us also go, that we may die with him." **(17)** Then when JESUS came, HE found that he had lain in the grave four days already. **(18)** Now Bethany was nigh unto Jerusalem, about fifteen furlongs off: **(19)** And many of the Jews came to Martha and Mary, to comfort them concerning their brother. **(20)** Then Martha, as soon as she haerd that JESUS was coming, went and met HIM: but Mary sat still in the house. **(21)** Then said Martha unto JESUS, "LORD, if THOU hadst been here, my brother had not died. **(22)** But I know, that even now, whatsoever wilt THOU ask of GOD, GOD will give it THEE." **(23)** JESUS saith unto her, "Thy brother shall rise again."

(24) Martha saith unto HIM, "I know that he shall rise again in the resurrection at the last day." (25) JESUS said unto her, "I AM the RESURRECTION, and the LIFE: he that believeth in ME, though he were dead, yet shall he live: (26) And whosoever liveth and believeth in ME shall never die. Believeth thou this? (27) She saith unto HIM, "Yea, LORD: I believe that THOU art the CHRIST, the SON of GOD, which should come into the world. (28) And when she had so said, she went her way, and called Mary her sister secretly, saying, "The MASTER is come, and calleth for thee. (29) As soon as she heard that, she arose quickly, and came unto HIM. (30) Now JESUS was not yet come into the town, but was in that place where Martha met HIM. (31) The Jews then which were with her in the house, and comforted her, when they saw Mary, that she rose up hastily and went out, followed her, saying, "She goeth unto the grave to weep there. (32) Then when Mary was come where JESUS was, and saw HIM, she fell down at HIS feet, saying unto HIM, "LORD, if THOU hadst been here, my brother had not died." (33) When JESUS therefore saw her weeping, and the Jews also weeping which came with her, HE groaned in the SPIRIT, and was troubled, (34) And said, "Where have ye laid him?" They said unto HIM, "LORD, come and see." (35) JESUS wept. (36) Then said the Jews, "Behold how HE loved him!" (37) And some of them said, "Could not this MAN, which opened the eyes of the blind, have caused that even this man should not have died?" (38) JESUS therefore again groaning in HIMSELF cometh to the grave. It was a cave, and a stone lay upon it. (39) JESUS said, "Take ye away the stone." Martha, the sister of him that was dead, saith unto HIM, "LORD, by this time he stinketh: for he has been dead four days. (40) JESUS said unto her, "Said I not unto thee, that, if thou wouldest believe, thou shouldest see the glory of GOD? (41) Then they took away the stone from the place where the dead was laid. And JESUS lifted up HIS eyes, and said, "FATHER, I thank THEE that THOU hast heard ME. (42) And I knew that THOU hearest ME always: but because of the people which stand by I said it, that they may belive that THOU hast sent ME." (43) And when HE thus had spoken, HE cried with a loud voice, "Lazarus, come forth." (44) And he that was dead came forth, bound hand and foot with graveclothes: and his face was bound about with a napkin. JESUS said unto them, "Loose him, and let him go."

COMMENTARY:

The sins of Adam and Eve ushered into the world, "physical death", and by contrast, the resurrection of CHRIST JESUS, ushered into the world, "spiritual life". "I AM the RESURRECTION and the LIFE" is the fifth of JESUS' seven great "I AM" statements that are found in the Gospel of John. The resurrection of CHRIST marked the start of a new age in human history that is still present today, because JESUS is still LORD over all of life, both the physical, and the spiritual.

When we accept the Eternal life that JESUS has to offer, the end of physical life becomes the beginning of a much more anticipated, spiritual life of eternity in Heaven in the glorious presence of the ALMIGHTY GOD. And so, in JESUS' resurrection we also see the birth of the "Christian Hope". Anyone who believes on JESUS already has "Eternal Life" (John 6:47).

In the gospel according to the Apostle John, in chapter 11, taking up at verse 17, we see JESUS arriving at Bethany some four days after HIS friends, Mary and Martha, had summoned HIM by messenger. They had sought JESUS out to tell HIM of the declining health of their brother Lazarus, who was also a close friend of JESUS'. They had wanted JESUS to hurry to Bethany so HE could heal their brother from what turned out to be a fatal sickness.

The day that JESUS got word of Lazarus' illness, HE informed HIS disciples that the illness would not result in a permanent demise, but rather, would be an event staged by GOD for HIS OWN glorification (v.4). And so they lingered on where they were for two more days before making the two-day journey to Bethany, just a few miles outside of Jerusalem.

When Martha got word that JESUS was near, she ran down the road to meet HIM. When she came to HIM she said to HIM, "LORD, if you had been here my brother would not have died. But even now I know that GOD will give YOU whatever YOU ask". Here we see in this statement by Martha, that, even in the short time since JESUS had begun HIS ministry, it had already become quite noticeable that nobody ever died while HE was around. It is a statement that was later echoed by her sister Mary, as soon as she came upon JESUS, at the burial site of her brother Lazarus.

We, as Christians, are all too well familiar with the ending to this, now famous, biblical account of what was then considered to be, JESUS' greatest miracle. "I AM the RESURRECTION and the LIFE" is what JESUS said to HIS friend Martha in John 11:25. For JESUS is LORD, over both, the "physical" and, the "spiritual" life. Our belief in HIM infuses in us a spiritual life that will persist, even after death.

That is why the greatest miracle of JESUS was not raising Lazarus back to the physical life, because we all know that, Mary and Martha's brother would again die. The greatest miracle, was, and is, in JESUS' power to grant endless spiritual life to those, who believe in HIM.

JESUS goes on to tell Martha that, "those who believe in HIM, even though they die like everyone else, will live again. They are given eternal life, just for believing in HIM, and will never die. And HE then asked HIS friend, "Did she believe?"

In John 11:27 Martha makes what I consider to be, one of the great "confession statements of faith" in all the annals of New Testament biblical history. Here she states, "I have always believed YOU are the MESSIAH, the SON of GOD, the ONE WHO has come into the world from GOD". Here she confesses three things about JESUS that are paramount to our understanding the theology of Christianity.

- First, we must understand that JESUS is the MESSIAH, WHO died on the cross at Golgotha for our sins.
- Secondly, we must know that HE is the SON of the LIVING GOD, and the most precious thing that GOD could give us as a sacrifice, simply because HE so loved the world that HE created.
- And finally, we must know that JESUS is the only ONE WHO has ever qualified as a perfect sacrifice, which is GOD's unwavering requirement for sin.

Salvation for us was the reason that GOD sent HIS only begotten SON into the world. JESUS had to be born of woman, so that HE could die for all mankind in general, and all Christians, in particular. This account of JESUS' raising Lazarus from the dead, back into the physical life, presents us with a perfect picture of what JESUS does spiritually for all who choose to believe in HIM. However, in our case, we will be raised into a spiritual eternal life, never to die again, as Lazarus would later do. And we will live in the very presence of the ALMIGHTY GOD in Heaven, as no doubt, Lazarus now is. We will be forever removed from the deadness of sin in this life, and placed into an eternity of love and joy with CHRIST JESUS, our LORD, in the life to come.

THE PLOT TO KILL JESUS
John 11:45-57

11 (45) Then many of the Jews which came to Mary, and had seen the things which JESUS did, believed on HIM. (46) But some of them went their ways to the Pharisees, and told them what things JESUS had done. (47) Then gathered the chief priests and the Pharisees a council, and said, "What do we? for this MAN doeth many miracles. (48) If we let HIM thus alone, all men, all men will believe on HIM: and the Romans shall come and take away both our place and nation." (49) And one of them, named Caiaphas, being the high priest that same year, said unto them, "Ye know nothing at all, (50) Nor consider that it is expedient for us, that one MAN should die for the people, and that the whole nation perish not." (51) And this spake he not of himself: but being high priest that year, he prophesied that JESUS should die for that nation; (52) And not for that nation only, but that also he should gather together in one the children of GOD that were scattered abroad. (53) Then from that day forth they took counsel together for to put HIM to death. (54) JESUS therefore walked no more openly among the Jews; but went thence unto a country near to the wilderness, into a city called Ephraim, and there continued with HIS disciples. (55) And the Jews' Passover was nigh at hand: and many went out of the country up to Jerusalem before the Passover, to purify themselves. (56) Then sought they for JESUS, and spake among themselves, as they stood in the temple, "What think ye, that HE will not come to the feast?" (57) Now both the chief priests and the Pharisees had given a commandment, that, "If any man knew where HE were, he should shew it, that they might take HIM."

COMMENTARY:

Although many of the people who witnessed JESUS' raising of Lazarus from the dead believed on HIM, there were still others who sided with the Sanhedrin. A few of those unbelievers quickly went and reported this miraculous event to the high priests and Pharisees at Jerusalem. The news was so disturbing to the religious hierarchy that they decided to call an emergency session. They feared that the Romans would react in an adverse way to this news and possibly destroy the temple, and maybe even, Jerusalem.

Normally, the position of high priest was a lifetime appointment, but in those days, the Romans appointed the high priest to his position, because they feared the power a man could gain by holding a position of that magnitude in Jerusalem for life. At that time, Caiaphas was the appointed high priest of the Romans. He served that position from A.D. 18 to A.D. 36. It was Caiaphas, whom GOD used to unwittingly prophecy that JESUS was to die a sacrificial death for the nations (John 11:49-52).

It was during that meeting that they officially issued an "All points bulletin" for the arrest of JESUS on sight (John 11:57). At this time JESUS decided to remove HIMSELF from public ministry, and went to the town of Ephraim, about fifteen miles north of Jerusalem, near the wilderness of Judea. There HE began HIS exclusive private teaching of HIS disciples, which continued up until the eve of HIS crucifixion.

When the time of the Passover came, many arrived early to go through the traditional cleansing process before the feast began. At that time there was much talk around Jerusalem, and especially in the temple, concerning the whereabouts of JESUS. Some, no doubt, wanted to hear HIM teach there, as HE had normally done, but, rest assuredly, there were others, who wanted to report HIM to the Pharisees so HE could be arrested.

WHAT DID WE LEARN FROM CHAPTER ELEVEN?
Here are some key points to remember

(1). Mary, the sister of Lazarus and Martha, was the Mary in scripture, who anointed CHRIST JESUS with expensive perfume for HIS pending burial. (John 11:1-2)

(2). Lazarus' death was for the glorification of CHRIST, by GOD the FATHER.

(3). By the time JESUS arrived at Bethany, Lazarus had been dead for four days. (John 11:17)

(4). JESUS' fifth "I AM statement" was spoken to HIS friend Martha. (John 11:25)

(5). John 11:35 is the shortest verse in the bible. It states that, "JESUS wept".

(6). JESUS' raising of Lazarus from the dead is the seventh sign of the Messiah.

(7). The high priest, Caiaphas, was used by GOD to unwittingly prophecy the sacrificial death of CHRIST JESUS for the nations. (John 11:49-52)

CHAPTER TWELVE:

JESUS ANOINTED AT BETHANY

SCRIPTURE:
The King James Version
John 12:1-11

12 (1) Then JESUS six days before the Passover came to Bethany, where Lazarus was which had been dead, whom HE raised from the dead. (2) There they made HIM a supper; and Martha served: but Lazarus was one of them that sat at the table with HIM (3) Then took Mary a pound of ointment of spikenard, very costly, and anointed the feet of JESUS, and wiped HIS feet with her hair: and the house was filled with the odour of the ointment. (4) Then said one of HIS disciples, Judas Iscariot, Simon's son, which should betray HIM, (5) "Why was not this ointment sold for three hundred pence, and given to the poor?" (6) This he said, not that he cared for the poor; but because he was a thief, and had the bag, and bare what was put therein. (7) Then said JESUS, "Let her alone: against the day of MY burying hath she kept this. (8) For the poor always ye have with you; but ME ye have not always." (9) Much people of the Jews therefore knew that HE was there: and they came not for JESUS' sake only, but that they might see Lazarus also, whom HE had raised from the dead. (10) But the chief priests consulted that they might put Lazarus also to death; (11) Because that by reason of him many of the Jews went away, and believed on JESUS.

COMMENTARY:

John chapter 12 marks the beginning of the last week of JESUS' life here on earth (HIS first advent). It was now just six days before the Passover, and HIS mission was almost complete. In a very few days HE would begin HIS "passion", and HE would suffer greatly for the likes of us. Salvation through CHRIST JESUS would soon be available for every human being who would ever again be born into this world. And we owe it all to GOD the FATHER, WHO loves us so much, that HE gave us the most precious part of HIMSELF, HIS only begotten SON, JESUS CHRIST, as a ransom for our sins.

The time schedule now becomes much more definite and critical, and here the occasion finds JESUS, once again, at the home of HIS friends Lazarus, Mary, and Martha. Here HE is being honored with a dinner that the women had so carefully and gratefully prepared. Lazarus, whom JESUS had recently given "a new lease on life", sat at the table with JESUS. It must have been a joyous time for the trio, and also for JESUS, and HE probably just wanted to spend a little quiet time with friends before HE continued on along HIS journey to Jerusalem, and, to HIS appointment with death on a hill called Golgotha.

All of a sudden, in the midst of the festive atmosphere of the moment, Mary walks in with an expensive bottle of precious ointment. She fell at the feet of JESUS and begin to anoint HIM with the aromatic fragrance of nard, which few Jews could afford at that time, without having to save for quite a while. It was usually sealed and imported from northern India in alabaster boxes or flasks, and was only opened on the most special of occasions. This lavish gift was perhaps meant by Mary, to be an expression of her deepest thanks to JESUS for HIS restoration of her brother's life, and, for simply being their friend and SAVIOR.

Unfortunately, one person's joy can often be another person's dislike, and now Judas, the traitor, shows us the first signs of his deceit and underlying greed. Judas was the treasurer of the group of the twelve disciples who regularly accompanied JESUS. And even though he speaks of using the proceeds from the sale of such a gift to feed the poor, John, who was also present at the table, knew that Judas only wanted control of the money for himself. For, he had regularly pilfered from the contents of their savings, and spent the money on himself (Vs. 4-6).

In verse 7, JESUS steps in to defend HIS friend Mary's actions toward HIM, and HE rebuked Judas and said, "Leave her alone. She did this in preparation for MY burial. You will always have the poor among you, but I will not be here with you much longer." And while they were there at the house in Bethany, many people came to see JESUS, and the man Lazarus, whom JESUS had raised from the dead. In fact, so popular had Lazarus become with the people, that, the Jewish hierarchy decided to kill him also. It was because of Lazarus' resurrection, that many people had abandoned the Pharisees and leading priests, and began to believe on JESUS.

THE TRIUMPHAL ENTRY
John 12:12-19

12 **(12)** On the next day much people that were come to the feast, when they heard that JESUS was coming to Jerusalem, **(13)** Took branches of palm trees, and went forth to meet HIM, and cried, "Hosanna: Blessed is the king of Israel that cometh in the name of the LORD" **(14)** And JESUS, when HE had found a young ass, sat thereon; as it is written, **(15)** "Fear not, daughter of Sion: behold, thy KING cometh, sitting on an ass's colt." **(16)** These things understood not HIS disciples at the first: but when JESUS was glorified, then remembered they that these things were written of HIM, and that they had done these things unto HIM. (17) The people therefore that was with HIM when HE called Lazarus out of his grave, and raised him from the dead, bare record. (18) For this cause the people also met HIM, for that they heard that HE had done this miracle. (19) The Pharisees therefore said among themselves, "Perceive ye how ye prevail nothing? Behold, the world is gone after HIM.

COMMENTARY:

All four Gospels (Matthew, Mark, Luke, and John) give an account of JESUS' triumphal final entry into Jerusalem. Here in John 12, verses 12-19, the scene shifts from that of a private dinner in the home of Lazarus, Mary, and Martha, to that of a noisy public parade on the streets of Jerusalem, that was fit for the most popular of kings. This event is significant in that, it is the only public demonstration of praise of HIMSELF that JESUS allowed while HE was ministering here on earth.

All of this commotion had come about as a result of JESUS' raising of Lazarus from the dead after he had lain in his tomb for four days in Bethany. JESUS' renewed popularity had put fear in the hearts of HIS enemies, the Pharisees, and they now felt for sure that a crisis was at hand. Little did they know that it was only GOD's way of forcing their hands, compelling them to act in the fulfilling of ancient prophesies. They were now to begin playing their roles in the final act of the salvation story, by successfully carrying out their plot to kill JESUS, by Roman method, on a cross at Golgotha.

As JESUS came, riding in on a young donkey (an act that symbolized peace), HIS disciples had not yet realized that it was also a fulfillment of prophecy. However, shortly after witnessing JESUS make HIS entrance into Jerusalem, they realized that once again, the scriptures concerning HIM had come to pass right before their eyes.

There were three groups of witnesses present that day in Jerusalem;

- First of all, there was the panic-stricken religious hierarchy, who, sought to kill JESUS, and perhaps Lazarus too. (For indeed, they were, by now, coming apart at the seams).
- Then, there were those people who had witnessed Lazarus' raising from the dead by CHRIST JESUS just a few days earlier.

- And finally, and, no doubt the largest group there, were those who had heard about the miracle concerning Lazarus, and had came to, perhaps, catch a glimpse of both he and JESUS.

But for whatever reason people were drawn to Jerusalem on that fateful day, the stage was now set for "the LAMB of GOD" to give HIS life, along with all the other Passover lambs that would be slain on the altar later in the week, for the sake of sinful man.

JESUS PREDICTS HIS DEATH
John 12:20-36

12 **(20)** And there were certain Greeks among them that came up to worship at the feast: **(21)** The same came therefore to Philip, which was of Bethsaida of Galilee, and desired him, saying, "Sir, we would see JESUS. **(22)** Philip cometh and telleth Andrew: and again Andrew and Philip tell JESUS. **(23)** And JESUS answered them, saying, "The hour is come, that the SON of Man should be glorified. **(24)** Verily, verily, I say unto you, Except a corn of wheat fall into the ground and die, it abideth alone: but if it die, it bringeth forth much fruit. **(25)** He that loveth his life shall lose it; and he that hateth his life in this world shall keep it unto life eternal. **(26)** If any man serve ME, let him follow ME; and where I AM, there shall also MY servant be: if any man serve ME, him will MY FATHER honour. **(27)** Now is MY soul troubled; and what shall I say? FATHER save ME from this hour; but for this cause came I unto this hour. **(28)** FATHER glorify THY name." Then came there a voice from Heaven, saying, "I have both glorified IT, and will glorify IT again." **(29)** The people therefore, that stood by, and heard it, said that it thundered: others said, "An angel spake to HIM". **(30)** JESUS answered and said, "This voice came not because of ME, but for your sakes. **(31)** Now is judgment of this world: now shall the prince of this world be cast out. **(32)** And I, if I be lifted up from the earth, will draw all men unto ME." **(33)** This HE said, signifying what death HE should die. **(34)** The people answered HIM, "We have heard out of the Law that CHRIST abideth forever: and how sayest THOU, "The SON of Man must be lifted up? WHO is this SON of Man?" **(35)** Then JESUS said unto them, "Yet a little while is the LIGHT with you. Walk while ye have the LIGHT, lest darkness come upon you: for he that walketh in darkness knoweth not whither he goeth. **(36)** While ye have LIGHT, believe in the LIGHT, that ye may be the children of LIGHT." These things spake JESUS, and departed, and did hide HIMSELF from them.

COMMENTARY:

A group of Greeks, who were, perhaps, "GOD-fearers", had come to the Passover to worship (v.20). GOD-fearers were "non-Jewish, uncircumcised believers in the GOD of Israel". They worshipped regularly in the Gentile court of the temple at Jerusalem, and also, would attend Jewish feasts, even though they had not yet become "Proselytes", or, "fully converted".

The original Greek text indicates that, this particular group of Greeks were "accustomed to come and worship at the feast". They probably approached Philip because of his Greek name, or, maybe they were familiar with him through his activities in the "Ten Cities" area of Galilee. But for whatever the reason may be, they desired greatly to speak personally with JESUS, and they chose Philip as a way of accomplishing that goal.

One of the resounding themes of the Gospel of John is that, JESUS is the SAVIOR of the whole world, not just the nation of Israel. John does not tell us whether or not JESUS spoke to this group in private, however, the response from JESUS when HE was told by Philip and Andrew that these men wanted to see HIM, contains truths that we can all use.

Here in this passage, JESUS sees beyond HIS suffering on the cross, and into the coming glory that would follow (John 12:23). Here HE uses the analogy of a "seed" to illustrate the great spiritual truth that "there can be no glory without suffering". There can also be "no fruitful life without death", or "no victory without surrender". A dead seed must be put in the ground before a fruitful plant can emerge. GOD's people are like seeds, tiny, and, in and of themselves, very insignificant. What makes us important is that, we have the life of GOD within us. However, it is a life that can never be fulfilled, until we surrender ourselves to GOD, and allow HIM, to sow us in the newness of life that came to us in the person of JESUS CHRIST. We must, alone, die to CHRIST, in order that we may live in fruitfulness for GOD. Those, who are willing, to follow JESUS in death, burial, and resurrection will be honored by GOD for all eternity.

As JESUS spoke, HE harbored a feeling of deep agitation at what was about to befall HIM regarding HIS hour of "passion". HE could have asked the FATHER to save HIM from what lay ahead in route to Calvary, but HE realized that that would defeat the whole purpose of HIS coming in the first place. And so, HE instead, asked the FATHER to glorify HIS name, through HIM.

Suddenly, the voice of GOD rang out from Heaven saying, "I have already brought glory, and I will do it again". The crowd, that had gathered, was divided on exactly what they had heard. The unbelievers were probably those who heard only the thunder, while the believers actually heard the voice of what they thought was an angel. At any rate, JESUS tells them that the voice was for their benefit, and not HIS.

JESUS then began to speak openly to the crowd about the cross, as HE informs them of a time of judgment for the world, and for satan, that had already arrived. HE would soon be "lifted up" on a cross so that all men, without distinction, would be drawn to HIM. The people were confused at JESUS' saying this, because, they had always understood that the MESSIAH would live forever, and now, here JESUS was, talking about how HE would die.

In verse 35, JESUS reminds them again, that, HE is the "LIGHT of the world". However, HE informs them also that HIS light would only shine for a limited time here on earth. We are responsible to take advantage of HIS LIGHT while we still can, so that we do not stumble into darkness later on, and will be able to, indeed, remain as children of GOD, living in the LIGHT, forevermore.

THE CONTINUED UNBELIEF OF THE PEOPLE
John 12:37-50

12 (37) But though HE had done so many miracles before them, yet they believed not on HIM: (38) That the saying of Esaias the prophet might be fulfilled, which he spake, "LORD who hath believed our report? And to whom hath the arm of the LORD been revealed? " (39) Therefore they could not believe, because that Esaias said again, (40) HE hath blinded their eyes, and hardened their heart; that they should not see with their eyes, nor understand with their heart, and be converted, and I should heal them. (41) These things said Esaias, when he saw HIS glory and spake of HIM. (42) Nevertheless among the chief rulers also many believed on HIM; but because of the Pharisees they did not confess HIM, lest they should be put out of the synagogue: (43) For they loved the praise of men more than the praise of GOD. (44) JESUS cried and said, "HE that believeth on ME, believeth not on ME, but on HIM that sent ME. (45) And he that seeth ME seeth HIM that sent ME. (46) I AM come a LIGHT into the world, that whosoever believeth on ME should not abide in darkness. (47) And if any man hear MY words, and believe not, I judge him not: for I came not to judge the world, but to save the world. (48) He that rejecteth ME, and receiveth not MY words, hath ONE that judgeth him: the word that I have spoken, the same shall judge him in the last day. (49) For I have not spoken of MYSELF; but the FATHER which sent ME, HE gave ME a commandment, what I should say, and what I should speak. (50) And I know that HIS commandment is life everlasting: whatsoever I speak therefore, even as the

FATHER said unto ME, so I speak.

COMMENTARY:

Despite all of the miraculous signs and wonders that JESUS had performed for almost three years now, most of the people still did not believe in HIM. The prophecy of Isaiah 53:1, and Isaiah 6:9-10, seemed to ring ever so true, as the final days of JESUS' ministry here on earth grinds to a dramatic conclusion. And even most of those, who did believe on JESUS, were hesitant to admit it, because they feared being expelled from the synagogue by the relentless Pharisees.

We see here in this passage, that the peoples' desire to obtain the praise of men, far exceeded, their desire to obtain the favor of GOD. It is hard for true Christians to phantom how this silent minority of believers could wholeheartedly believe in JESUS, and yet, show so much concern for the opinion of JESUS' opposition, the Pharisees.

In verses 44-50, JESUS addresses the crowd for the final time. HE tells them that, if they trust in HIM, they are really trusting in GOD, WHO sent HIM, and that, when they see HIM, they are actually seeing GOD the FATHER. JESUS reiterates HIS claim of being the "LIGHT OF THE WORLD", WHO came to shine in the darkness so that all who put their trust in HIM, and follow HIM, would no longer remain in darkness. HE also tells them, that, anyone who hears HIM and doesn't obey HIM will not be judged by HIM on this occasion.

On this occasion, JESUS' first advent, HE only came to save, however, all who reject HIM and HIS message will be judged at the "day of judgment" by the very words that HE was now speaking to them. At that time, HE was only delivering the message of GOD, WHO sent HIM, which instructs them how to live this life, so that they can have eternal life with GOD in Heaven, as opposed to living in eternal damnation in Hell.

In JESUS, every human being is confronted by GOD HIMSELF. To listen to HIM is to listen to GOD, and to see HIM, is to see GOD. Through CHRIST JESUS, GOD comes face to face with man, and man, thereby, comes face to face with GOD. It is a confrontation that can culminate in only two distinctive outcomes, and both are found at the very heart of judgment:

- The first is, that, any man, who can come face to face with JESUS, and remain completely unaffected by HIS presence, the same, would also be impervious to GOD HIMSELF. Thereby, that person, unwittingly, has already judged himself.

- The second scenario gives us this picture, as JESUS says, in effect, that, anyone who rejects HIM and HIS message now, will, in the last day, be judged, by the truth of the very words that they have already heard HIM speak, and ignored.

WHAT DID WE LEARN FROM CHAPTER TWELVE?
Here are some key points to remember

(1). JESUS begins the final week of HIS ministry at the home of HIS friends Lazarus, Mary, and Martha. (John 12:1)

(2). Mary anoints JESUS with expensive perfume, in preparation for HIS burial. (John 12:3-7)

(3). Judas Iscariot, who later betrayed JESUS, objects to the anointing. (John 12:4-6)

(4) JESUS received a hero's welcome, upon HIS final entry into Jerusalem. (John 12:12-19)

(5). The religious leaders of Jerusalem also sought to kill JESUS' friend, Lazarus, whom JESUS had earlier, raised from the dead. (John 12:10-11)

(6). To have faith in JESUS is to have faith in GOD. (John 12:44)

(7). Don't let anything keep you from professing your faith in CHRIST. (John 12:42-50)

CHAPTER THIRTEEN:

(81)

JESUS WASHES HIS DISCIPLE'S FEET

SCRIPTURE:
The King James Version
John 13:1-17

13 (1) Now before the feast of the Passover, when JESUS knew that HIS hour was come that HE should depart out of this world unto the FATHER, having loved HIS OWN which were in the world, HE loved them unto the end. (2) And supper being ended, the devil having now put into the heart of Judas Iscariot, Simon's son, to betray HIM; (3) JESUS knowing that the FATHER had given all things into HIS hands, and that HE was come from GOD, and went to GOD; (4) HE riseth from supper, and laid aside HIS garments; and took a towel, and girded HIMSELF. (5) after that HE poureth water into a basin, and began to wash the disciples' feet, and to wipe them with the towel wherewith HE was girded. (6) Then cometh HE to Simon Peter: and Peter saith unto HIM, "LORD, dost THOU wash my feet?" (7) JESUS answered and said unto him, "What I do thou knoweth not now; but thou shalt know hereafter." (8) Peter saith unto HIM, "THOU shalt never wash my feet." JESUS answered him, "If I wash thee not, thou hast no part with ME." (9) Simon Peter saith unto HIM, "LORD, not my feet only, but also my hands and my head." (10) JESUS saith to him, "He that is washed needeth not save to wash his feet, but is clean every whit: and ye are clean, but not all." (11) For HE knew who should betray HIM; therefore said HE, "Ye are not all clean." (12) So after HE had washed their feet, and had taken HIS garments, and was set down again, HE said unto them, "Know ye what I have done to you? (13) Ye call ME MASTER and LORD: and ye say well; for so I AM. (14) If I then, your LORD and MASTER, have washed your feet; ye also ought to wash one another's feet. (15) For I have given you an example, that ye should do as I have done to you. (16) Verily, verily, I say unto you, The servant is not greater than his lord; neither he that is sent greater than he that sent him. (17) If ye know these things, happy are ye if ye do them.

COMMENTARY:

The Gospel of John gives us the most complete details of JESUS' instructions to HIS disciples on the eve of HIS crucifixion. Chapters 13-17 represent a concentrated dose of JESUS' private teachings to HIS select group of disciples on the night of HIS arrest. HE begins the evening with the surprising act of washing HIS disciple's feet, one disciple at a time. It was an endearing and humble effort on JESUS' part, to express to HIS closest followers, the kind of brotherly love that HE had in HIS heart for each of them.

JESUS knew that HIS time to depart from this world was drawing ever closer, and, that HIS death on the cross was now imminent. The devil had already entered into the heart of Judas Iscariot and enticed him to go forward with his plan of betrayal against JESUS. And now, the stage was set for the "passion of CHRIST" to begin. But first, there would still be time for some intimate instructions from the MAN WHO had come to mean so much to this unwitting, rag-tagged group of simple and untrained men. And the first of HIS instructions was aimed at teaching them to serve each other in the most menial of ways, which was, in this case, washing each other's feet.

After washing their feet, JESUS put HIS robe back on and sat down and asked what they had learned from what HE had just done. HE told HIS faithful that they always called HIM MASTER and LORD, and that they were correct in doing so. However, if HE, as their MASTER, would wash their feet, how much more willing should they be to wash each other's feet?

JESUS had given HIS disciples an example and HE wanted them to follow suit with their treatment toward each other. And, even though a servant is never greater than his master, and a messenger is never more important than the one who sent him, JESUS, WHO is MASTER over all mankind, came to serve all mankind, perfectly representing HIS FATHER GOD, WHO sent HIM into the world that HE so loved.

All the way up until the very hour of Judas' betrayal of JESUS, he had been, protected by JESUS from being discovered by the other disciples. JESUS knew from the beginning what role Judas would portray in the outcome of HIS ministry, but HE in no way compelled him to play it. Instead, HE exposed Judas to all of the privileges that HE had afforded the other disciples, and yet Judas' sinful heart remained unchanged by JESUS' presence.

It is like the professed Christian in the church today, who might attend church every weekend, and go to Sunday school, midweek bible study, participate in church ministries etc., and never really, in their heart, accept CHRIST for WHO HE is, as our LORD and SAVIOR.

JESUS PREDICTS HIS BETRAYAL
John 13:18-30

13 (18) "I speak not of you all: I know whom I have chosen: but that the scripture may be fulfilled, he that eateth bread with ME hath lifted up his heel against ME. (19) Now I tell you before it come, that, when it is come to pass, ye may believe that I AM HE. (20) Verily, verily, I say unto you, He that receiveth whomsoever I send receiveth ME; and he that receiveth ME receiveth HIM that sent ME." (21) When JESUS had thus said, HE was troubled in spirit, and testified, and said, "Verily, verily, I say unto you, that one of you shall betray ME." (22) Then the disciples looked one on another, doubting of whom HE spake. (23) Now there was leaning on JESUS' bosom one of HIS disciples, whom JESUS loved. (24) Simon Peter therefore beckoned to HIM, that he should ask who it should be of whom HE spake. (25) He then lying on JESUS' breast saith unto HIM, LORD, who is it? (26) JESUS answered, "He it is, to whom I shall give a sop, when I have dipped it." And when HE had dipped the sop, HE gave it to Judas Iscariot, the son of Simon. (27) And after the sop satan entered into him. Then said JESUS unto him, "That thou doest, do quickly." (28) Now no man at the table knew for what intent HE spake this unto him. (29) For some of them thought, because Judas had the bag, that JESUS had said unto him, Buy those things that we have need of against the feast; or, that he should give something to the poor. (30) He then having received the sop went immediately out: and it was night.

COMMENTARY:

The "Last Supper" took place on a Thursday night, and the theme of that dinner was a theme of "Love". After JESUS performed the menial act of foot washing to HIS disciples, HE now decides, with a heavy heart, that it is time to expose the one who would betray HIM. It would be one of those very men whose feet HE had just washed.

In verse 18 of this passage, JESUS' allusion to Psalms 41:9, where King David laments his betrayal by his trusted friend, Ahithophel, who like Judas, ultimately committed suicide by hanging (2 Samuel 17:23), clearly identifies this incident as being prophetic. What had happened to David was now happening to David's greater SON, JESUS CHRIST.

When JESUS mentioned the fact that one of them would betray HIM, the disciples were stunned, and began to look upon each other, wondering which of them could be capable of doing such a terrible thing. Peter motioned to John, who sat next to JESUS, and asked him to ask JESUS who it would be. JESUS answered, apparently only to John's hearing, that it would be the one HE gave the bread dipped in sauce to, which turned out to be Judas Iscariot, the son of Simon.

Immediately, upon eating the bread, satan entered into Judas, and he was sent away by JESUS to perform his act of treason. None of the others at the table comprehended what JESUS meant, especially since Judas was treasurer of the group, and, at the time, had been sitting in the position of honor at JESUS' side. They felt for certain that JESUS was sending him away to do something honorable like purchasing food for the Passover, or making a donation to the poor.

However, Judas had already made his deal with the religious leaders to betray JESUS on that night, and JESUS' statement to him to "Go and do it quickly" let Judas know that HE knew of his plan. And so, at that point, JESUS was, in effect, giving Judas a final chance to repent. Unfortunately, Judas' heart was all set to go forward with this final rejection of CHRIST JESUS, and the rest, is the tragic history of a fallen soul.

After Judas had left the room, JESUS began again, speaking to the eleven disciples that remained. HE tells them that HIS time has come to enter into HIS glory, and that GOD would also receive glory through HIM, because of it. JESUS' glory was to be revealed in HIS death, and thereby, GOD would also glorify HIMSELF.

JESUS PREDICTS PETER'S DENIAL
John 13:31-38

13 (31) Therefore, when he was gone out, JESUS said, "Now is the SON of MAN glorified, and GOD is glorified in HIM. (32) If GOD be glorified in HIM, GOD shall also glorify HIM in HIMSELF, and shall straightway glorify HIM. (33) Little children, yet a little while I AM with you. Ye shall seek ME: and as I said unto the Jews, "Whither I go, ye cannot come;" so now I say to you. (34) A new commandment I give unto you, "That ye love one another;" as I have loved you, that ye also love one another. (35) By this shall all men know that ye are MY disciples, if ye have love one to another." (36) Simon Peter said unto HIM, "LORD, whither goest THOU? JESUS answered him, "Whither I go, thou canst not follow ME now; but shall follow ME afterwards." (37) Peter said unto HIM, "LORD, why cannot I follow THEE now? I will lay down my life for THY sake." (38) JESUS answered, "Wilt thou lay down thy life for MY sake? Verily, verily, I say unto thee, "The cock shall not crow, till thou hast denied ME thrice."

COMMENTARY:

The term, "little children", that, is expressed by JESUS in verse 38, shows us the deep concern HE had for HIS beloved disciples' well-being after HIS departure. HE knew that they could survive HIS absence, only if they obeyed HIS teachings and HIS commandment to love. Here, in this passage, is the only time in scripture that JESUS uses this term. Nevertheless, it is a term that seemed to stick with the apostle John over the years, as we see him use it often in his first letter to the Christians who were dear to him.

JESUS now reiterates a statement HE had earlier made to the Jewish leaders, that, "where HE was about to go, they could not follow". This statement, of JESUS' leaving them, perhaps, more than anything else, deeply troubled the hearts of the disciples. Certainly it must have set off a whirlwind of perplexing questions in their minds and hearts. And right in the midst of their confusion, JESUS delivers to them, the one and only new commandment, that, HE would ever give, during HIS ministry. It is a commandment that also comes to us today, from across the spans of time, in hopes that we too, can perform it also in our lives. It is the commandment to "love each other, just as JESUS has loved us".

Love is the Christian image of the family, and it was to take on a new meaning and power, because of the death of CHRIST JESUS. And with the coming of the HOLY SPIRIT to aid us, love would have a new power in our lives. It would stand as undeniable evidence as to whether we are true followers of our LORD and SAVIOR, JESUS CHRIST.

However, still stuck on the statement of JESUS' leaving, Peter steps forward and insists that wherever JESUS was going, he was fully ready to follow, right then. In fact, Peter not only insisted that he was ready to follow JESUS wherever HE might go, but he was also ready to lay down his life for HIM. And just when Peter thought that he could not be hit with a more disturbing statement than the one of JESUS' leaving them, our LORD and SAVIOR hits him with an, even more, heart-troubling declaration. HE prophecies to HIS bewildered disciple, that, "before the rooster crows tomorrow morning, you will have already denied knowing ME, three times."

WHAT DID WE LEARN FROM CHAPTER THIRTEEN?
Here are some key points to remember

(1). JESUS showed the disciples the full extent of HIS love, through the menial task of washing HIS disciples feet. (John 13:1)

(2). The symbolic link of "foot-washing" reminds us of our continued need for cleansing from sin, even during our Christian walk. (John 13:8)

(3). Our spiritual bodies are cleansed when we let JESUS into our lives to help us transform our hearts, but we need continuous cleansing of our spiritual feet from sin, during our Christian walk. (John 13:10)

(4). If we are to follow CHRIST we must take on the attitude of a servant. (John 13:14-15)

(5). The grip of satan, can only tighten on those who make the decision to reject JESUS' final offer of salvation. (John 13:26-27)

(6). Psalms 41:9, which refers to David's betrayal by Ahithophel (2 Samuel 16:15-17:23), parallels the event of JESUS' OWN betrayal, by Judas Iscariot. (John 13:18)

(7). JESUS commands us to love each other, as HE HIMSELF has loves us. This action will be used to identify those who follow HIM. (John 13:34-35)

CHAPTER FOURTEEN:

JESUS, THE WAY OF LIFE

SCRIPTURE:
The King James Version
John 14:1-14

14 **(1)** Let not your heart be troubled: ye believe in GOD, believe also in ME. **(2)** In MY FATHER's house are many mansions: if it were not so, I would have told you. I go to prepare a place for you. **(3)** And if I go and prepare a place for you, I will come again, and receive you unto MYSELF; that where I AM, there ye may be also. **(4)** And whither I go ye know, and the way ye know." **(5)** Thomas said unto HIM, "LORD, we know not whither YOU goest; and how can we know the way?" **(6)** JESUS saith unto him, "I AM the WAY, the TRUTH, and the LIFE: no man cometh unto the FATHER, but by ME. **(7)** If ye had known ME, ye should have known MY FATHER also; and from henceforth ye know HIM, and have seen HIM." **(8)** Philip saith unto HIM, "LORD, shew us the FATHER, and it will sufficeth us." **(9)** JESUS saith unto him, "Have I been so long time with you, and yet hast thou not known ME, Philip? He that hath seen ME hath seen the FATHER; and how sayest thou then, "Shew us the FATHER?" **(10)** Believest thou not that I AM in the FATHER, and the FATHER in ME? The words that I speak unto you I speak not of MYSELF: but the FATHER that dwelleth in ME, HE doeth the works. **(11)** Believe ME that I AM in the FATHER, and the FATHER in ME: or else believe ME for the very works' sake. **(12)** Verily, verily, I say unto you, He that believeth on ME, the works that I do shall he do also; and greater works than these shall he do; because I go unto MY FATHER. **(13)** And whatsoever ye shall ask in MY name, that will I do, that the FATHER may be glorified in the SON. **(14)** If ye shall ask any thing in MY name, I will do it.

COMMENTARY:

In John chapter 14 JESUS continues to teach HIS disciples in private. Here HE focuses on trying to encourage them to hold fast to the belief that HE has revealed to them exactly what GOD THE FATHER is like. In the Greek, the word New Testament writers use for "promise" is "epaggello" (ep-ang-el-ee-ah), and it is "an announcement of divine assurance of good".

John 14:1-3 is arguably, one of the most beautifully written passages in, perhaps, the most beautifully written book, in all of Scripture. It comes in the form of a "divine promise" to those who believe in CHRIST JESUS. Here in this passage, JESUS, first, encourages, and then, makes a promise to HIS followers with these divine words; "Let not your heart be troubled: ye believe in GOD, believe also in ME. In MY FATHER's house are many mansions: if it were not so, I would tell you. I go to prepare a place for you. And if I go and prepare a place for you, I will come again, and receive you unto MYSELF; that where I AM, there ye may be also" (KJV).

It is a promise that is made at a time when the cumulative weight and effect of all the previous revelations that JESUS had laid on HIS disciples had begun to set in and depress them. Remember, HE had already revealed to them that HE would go away, and, they would not be able to follow HIM (John 7:34, 8:21, 12:8 & 35, and 13:33). HE had also revealed to them that HE would die (John 12:32-33), and, that one of them would betray HIM (John 13:21). Furthermore, HE had already revealed to Peter that he would deny HIM, not once, but three times before daybreak (John 13:38). And also, that satan would be working against them (Luke 22:31-32), and, at that time, everyone of them would fall away from HIM (Matthew 26:31).

And so we see it is a statement that was much needed to try and comfort and allay the fears of what was about to befall HIS disciples in the very near future. It is said that a person's heart is at the center of their personality, and that, we must keep our hearts with all diligence. Our soul's sorrow is relieved when we trust in the word of GOD, and CHRIST says, if you trust GOD, trust also in HIM.

"I AM the WAY, THE TRUTH, and THE LIFE" is what JESUS said to a "doubting" Thomas in John 14:6. It is the sixth of JESUS' seven great "I AM statements" found in the Gospel of John. JESUS tells us plainly that if we have seen HIM, we have already seen GOD, and if we "know" HIM and "have" HIM in us, we already possess "Eternal Life".

In the final analysis, all man ever really seeks is a better life for himself and his family. He never seeks knowledge, just for knowledge sake, but rather, for what that knowledge can do to make his life more worth living. It is JESUS' claim, that obedience to HIM is the only true foundation that we can securely build upon. It is HIS contention that life through HIM is the only life worth living. No one can go to the FATHER, but by JESUS, because, HE alone, is "THE WAY" to GOD. In HIM, we see exactly what GOD is like. And only HE can usher us, into GOD's OWN glorious presence, without fear, without guilt, and, without shame.

Anyone who believes in CHRIST JESUS will desire to do the same work that HIS earthly ministry demonstrates to us that HE did. But JESUS says that we can do even greater works than HE did, and this is simply because many of us will have much more time on this earth than HE had. In addition, we are able to ask GOD for anything within HIS Will, and, in the name of JESUS, and HE will grant it, because all of JESUS' work during HIS earthly ministry, brought glory to HIS FATHER in Heaven (Vs. 12-14). And if we do the work of CHRIST JESUS, we too, will bring glory the SAME, our FATHER, WHO art in Heaven.

THE PROMISE OF THE HOLY SPIRIT
John 14:15-31

14 **(15)** "If ye love ME keep MY commandments. **(16)** And I will pray the FATHER, and HE shall give you another COMFORTER, that HE may abide in you forever; **(17)** Even the SPIRIT of TRUTH; WHOM the world cannot receive, because it seeth HIM not, neither knoweth HIM: but ye know HIM; for HE dwelleth with you, and shall be in you. **(18)** I will not leave you comfortless: I will come to you. **(19)** Yet a little while, and the world seeth ME no more; but ye see ME: because I live, ye shall live also. **(20)** At that day ye shall know that I AM in MY FATHER, and ye in ME, and I in you. **(21)** HE that hath MY commandments, and keepeth them, he it is that loveth ME: and he that loveth ME shall be loved of MY FATHER, and I will love him, and will manifest MYSELF to him." **(22)** Judas said unto HIM, not Iscariot, "LORD, how is it that THOU wilt manifest THYSELF unto us, and not unto the world?" **(23)** JESUS answered and said unto him, "If a man love ME, he will keep MY words: and MY FATHER will love him, and WE will come unto him, and make our abode with him. **(24)** He that loveth ME not keepeth not MY sayings: and the word which ye hear is not mine, but the FATHER's which sent ME. **(25)** These things have I spoken unto you, being yet present with you. **(26)** But the COMFORTER, which is the HOLY GHOST, WHOM the FATHER will send in MY name, HE shall teach you all things, and bring all things to your remembrance, whatsoever I have said unto you. **(27)** Peace I leave with you, MY peace I give unto you: not as the world giveth, give I unto you. Let not your heart be troubled, neither let it be afraid. **(28)** Ye have heard how I said unto you, I go away, and come again unto you. If ye loved ME, ye would rejoice, because I said, I go unto the FATHER: for MY FATHER is greater than I. **(29)** And now I have told you before it come to pass, that, when it is come to pass, ye might believe. (30) Hereafter I will not talk much with you: for the prince of this world cometh, and hath nothing in ME. (31) But that the world may know that I love the FATHER; and as the FATHER gave ME commandment, even so I do. Arise, let us go hence."

COMMENTARY:

John 14:15-31 is the conclusion of JESUS', now famous, "Upper Room Discourse" to HIS disciples. Up until this point, very little had been mentioned, regarding the HOLY SPIRIT. In the New Testament Greek, the word used for "Comforter" is "Parakletos" (Par-ak-lay-tos), and it is "an Intercessor", or "a Counselor". "Comforter" is the word translated here and used by JESUS to describe the function of the HOLY SPIRIT, WHOM HE would send soon after HIS departure back into Heaven. This COMFORTER would stand as a force against man's own "sin nature" and would lead him into all truth. HE would also be a force that "unbelievers" would not be able to see or receive into their lives. Only those, who receive CHRIST first, will be able to partake in this wonderful gift from GOD the FATHER.

And while the SPIRIT of GOD was now dwelling with the disciples in the person of CHRIST JESUS, HE would later come to "indwell" anyone who chose to follow JESUS through the cross. This type of reaction on people by the HOLY SPIRIT would be different from the way HE came upon people and inspired them in the Old Testament times. In those days, the HOLY SPIRIT would come upon people for a period, and then, would leave them. However, this time which JESUS is speaking of here in this passage (that time of the first "Pentecost"), will be a time when the HOLY SPIRIT would come to dwell in the body of the Christian Believer forever.

The HOLY SPIRIT is intended to actually fulfill the role of JESUS HIMSELF, in the lives of those, who believe on HIM. It was JESUS' way of not abandoning us like orphans, and leaving us at the mercy of satan and his demons, who, of course, have no mercy. That is why, the way we treat the HOLY SPIRIT is the way we treat CHRIST JESUS. When we accept JESUS into our lives, our bodies become the temple of the HOLY SPIRIT, and since the HOLY SPIRIT wrote the Word of GOD, the way we treat GOD's Word (the Bible) is the way we treat GOD in HIS fullness.

Our love of GOD is shown by our willingness to obey CHRIST through the prompting of the HOLY SPIRIT, which seeks to guide us into all righteousness. GOD the FATHER, GOD the SON, and GOD the HOLY SPIRIT are indeed ONE and inseparable. JESUS left us with a peace of mind and heart that cannot be found in the world. And we can now come to rest in the thought, that, this life is by no means, the final act of the human drama.

WHAT DID WE LEARN FROM CHAPTER FOURTEEN?
Here are some key points to remember

(1). Our trust in GOD is the antidote to a troubled heart. (John 14:1)

(2). JESUS went to prepare a place for believers in the Kingdom of Heaven. (John 14:2-3)

(3). "I AM the WAY, the TRUTH, and the LIFE" is the sixth of JESUS' seven great "I AM" statements. (John 14:6)

(4). When we pray, we should pray our prayers in JESUS' name. (John 14:13)

(5). The HOLY SPIRIT dwells in all those who believe on CHRIST JESUS. (John 14:15-17)

(6). "Obedience" is considered by GOD to be a "love response". (John 14:21 & 23-24)

(7). The HOLY SPIRIT is our living link to CHRIST JESUS. (John 14:26)

CHAPTER FIFTEEN:

JESUS, THE TRUE VINE

SCRIPTURE:
The King James Version
John 15:1-17

15 (1) "I AM the true vine, and MY FATHER is the HUSBANDMAN. (2) Every branch in ME that beareth not fruit HE taketh away: and every branch that beareth fruit, HE purgeth it, that it may bring forth more fruit. (3) Now ye are clean through the word which I have spoken unto you. (4) Abide in ME, and I in you. As the branch cannot bear fruit of itself, except it abide in the vine; no more can ye, except ye abide in ME. (5) I AM the vine, ye are the branches: He that abideth in ME, and I in him, the same bringeth forth much fruit: for without ME ye can do nothing. (6) If a man abide not in ME, he is cast forth as a branch, and is withered; and men gather them, and cast them into the fire, and they are burned. (7) If ye abide in ME, and MY words abide in you, ye shall ask what ye will, and it shall be done unto you. (8) Herein is MY FATHER glorified, that ye bear much fruit; so shall ye be MY disciples. (9) As the FATHER hath loved ME, so have I loved you: continue ye in MY love. (10) If ye keep MY commandments, ye shall abide in MY love; even as I have kept MY FATHER's commandments, and abide in HIS love. (11) These things have I spoken unto you, that MY joy might remain in you, and that your joy might be full. (12) This is MY commandment, "That ye love one another, as I have loved you." (13) Greater love hath no man than this, that a man lay down his life for his friends. (14) Ye are MY friends, if ye do whatsoever I command you. (15) Henceforth I call you not servants; for the servant knoweth not what his LORD doeth: bit I have called you friends; for all things that I have heard of MY FATHER I have made known unto you. (16) Ye have not chosen ME, but I have chosen you, and ordained you, that ye should go and bring forth fruit, and that your fruit should remain: that whatsoever ye shall ask of the FATHER in MY name, HE may give it to you. (17) These things I command you, that ye love one another.

COMMENTARY:

Throughout the Old Testament, the analogy of the "vineyard" is used as a depiction of GOD's beloved Israel. However, this term is never used apart from the idea of degeneration. The descriptions by Isaiah (Isaiah 5:1-7), Jeremiah (Jeremiah

2:21-22), Ezekiel (Ezekiel 15 & 19:10-14), Hosea (Hosea 10:1), and King David (Psalm 80:8-13) all stress the point of degeneration, or, a moral decline of GOD's chosen people (the church).

In John 15:1-16:4, the author of GOD writes of JESUS' instructions to HIS Disciples, that they should be "rightly related" to HIM, to each other as Christians (15:11-17), and, to the World of Unbelievers (15:18-16:4).

Christians are to have three respective duties. They are to;

- Abide in JESUS (Vs.1-10)
- Love each other (Vs.11-17)
- Witness and testify to the World (Vs.18-16:4)

"I am the True Vine" is the last of the seven, now famous, "I am" statements of our LORD and SAVIOR, JESUS CHRIST that are found in the Gospel according to Saint John. The scene in this particular passage, takes place on the eve of JESUS' trials and subsequent Crucifixion, by Roman method. Here JESUS seeks to relate and demonstrate to HIS Disciples, and to us, just what GOD THE FATHER, and HE HIMSELF, expects from HIS followers as Christians living in the world.

JESUS, as the "True Vine", fulfills that which GOD had intended for the Israelites and the world in general. GOD is the Cultivator and Protector of all of life, human and otherwise, and HE desires good fruit, from each of us. In fact, we see JESUS stressing that point in 15:2-16, no less than eight times. The fruit, which GOD expects from the human side of HIS creation, is obedience, righteousness, and justice.

JESUS tells us that every branch, or person in this case, that does not produce good fruit will be cut off from HIS vine. Here we see that, every person (branch), who professes to be a follower of CHRIST, is not necessarily a "true follower", or "a producing branch" of "THE TRUE VINE". Such branches, or people, will be cut off from THE TRUE VINE in the last day, or in the "time of harvest". The great example of this is Judas Iscariot. Although Judas Iscariot was a branch of THE TRUE VINE, he was not a producing branch, or true follower. He did not produce good fruit, and therefore, had to be cut off from THE TRUE VINE, and burned in the end.

In the Greek, the word the Apostle John, and other New Testament writers use for "remain" is "meno" (men-o), and it means "to stay in a given place, state of mind, relationship, or expectancy"; and "to abide, continue, dwell, or endure". This word occurs 11 times in this particular chapter of this Gospel account of John. The fruitfulness, of which JESUS speaks of in this passage, can only occur, as a result of HIS life being reproduced in ours.

In other words, our life and behavior must reflect JESUS' life and behavior, and we must "remain" in HIM, or "continue" to reflect HIS image to others, through our own behavior, throughout our entire lifetimes. We, as Christians, must prove to the world, through our behavior, that Christianity really does produce the best men and women.

It is only by doing this, can we be considered as "true followers", or "producing branches" of the "TRUE VINE" of GOD. If we remain, or abide in JESUS, we will continue to bear good fruit. If we fail to remain in JESUS (on the VINE), in spite of all of GOD's tender loving care of the vineyard, we will be lopped off, and cast into the fire to burn as useless wood.

In John 15:11-17, JESUS moves on to instruct HIS disciples (and us), as to how we should "rightly relate to each other" as Christians. Here, we see JESUS delivering to all who seek to follow HIM, the only commandment that HE would ever give, and it is to "Love one another, as I have loved you" (John 15:12). It is a commandment that the Apostle John never forgot.

According to Jewish folklore, the Apostle John, who lived longer than all of JESUS' original twelve Disciples, in his old age, had to be carried into the Temple, because he could no longer walk. At that time, the Apostle's sermon consisted of only one sentence, "Little children, love one another". It is one of the more lovely stories in a Biblical Church history that consists of countless lovely stories from the early Church. Every time I think of it, it nearly brings me to tears.

THE WORLD'S HATRED OF CHRISTIANS
John 15:18-16:4

15 (18) "If the world hate you, ye know that it hated ME before it hated you. (19) If ye were of the world, the world would love his own: but because ye are not of the world, but I have chosen you out of the world, therefore the world hateth you. (20) Remember the word that I said unto you, "The servant is not greater than his lord. If they have persecuted ME, they will also persecute you; If they have kept MY saying, they will keep yours also. (21) But all these things will they do unto you for MY name's sake, because they know not HIM that sent ME. (22) If I had not come and spoken unto them, they had not had sin: but now they have no cloke for their sin. (23) He that hateth ME hateth MY FATHER also. (24) If I had not done among them the works which none other man did, they had not had sin: but now have they both seen and hated both ME and MY FATHER. (25) But this cometh to pass, that the word might be fulfilled that is written in their law, "They hated ME without a cause". (26) But when the COMFORTER is come, WHOM I will send unto you from the FATHER, even the SPIRIT of TRUTH, which preceedeth from the FATHER, HE shall testify of ME: (27) And ye also shall bear witness, because ye have been with ME from the beginning."

16 (1) These things I have spoken unto you, that ye should not be offended. (2) They shall put you out of the synagogues: yea, the time cometh, that whosoever killeth you wil think that he doeth GOD service. (3) And these things will they do unto you, because they have not known the FATHER, nor ME. (4) But these things have I told you, that when the time shall come, ye may remember that I told you of them. And these things I said not unto you at the beginning, because I was with you.

COMMENTARY:

In John 15:18-16:4, JESUS instructs us on how we should relate to the world. When we choose the Christian walk, we automatically become strangers to worldly behavior. We are no longer permanent residents of this earth, but rather, we become citizens of Heaven, and therefore, the laws of GOD should become paramount to us.

Here in this passage, JESUS warns of the hatred that the World will have for those who follow HIM. As long as a person belongs to the World, the World will always love that person. That is primarily because that person resembles the World through his or her behavior, and to hate that person, would, quite literally, mean hating themselves.

The person who hates the true Christian, hates JESUS, and thereby, hates GOD. Anyone, who is shown the Word of GOD, and does not accept it, is guilty of denying CHRIST, who is the "personification" of the Word of GOD, and therefore, is GOD. We as Christians have a duty to go out into the world and share the Gospel with dignity and respect. JESUS empowered us with the HOLY SPIRIT, and GOD goes before us, to prepare the hearts of those to whom we may be speaking. "Be of good cheer", and "be not afraid" is what JESUS said to Peter and HIS other Disciples that day in far off Palestine, where HE "walked on water", in order to give them encouragement to "remain in HIM".

We are called to go out into the world, and we don't have to be afraid. JESUS will always come to us, from across the storms of life, but we must continue to bear good fruit, by remaining in HIM. If we fail to bear good fruit, as Judas Iscariot failed to, we will be cut off from the "TRUE VINE" that brings with it, Eternal Life.

JESUS eternally encourages us through these immortal words that HE spoke to HIS closest disciples, just prior to HIS ascension back into HIS Heavenly Realm; "Go ye therefore, and teach all nations, baptizing them in the name of the FATHER, and of the SON, and of the HOLY GHOST: Teaching them to observe all things whatsoever I have commanded you: and, lo, I AM with you always, even unto the end of the world" (Matthew 28:19-20 - KJV).

WHAT DID WE LEARN FROM CHAPTER FIFTEEN?
Here are some key points to remember

(1). "I AM the TRUE VINE" is the last of the seven great "I AM" statements made by JESUS in the Gospel of John.

(2). Christians are to be rightly related to CHRIST JESUS. (John 15:1-11)

(3). Christians are to be rightly related to each other. (John 15:12-17)

(4). Christians are to be rightly related to the world. (John 15: 18-27)

(5). Remember how JESUS measures friendship. (John 15:13-15)

(6). We are commanded by JESUS to love each other as HE loves us. (John 15:12)

(7). Worldly people will hate you because you belong to CHRIST JESUS. (John 15:21)

CHAPTER SIXTEEN:

THE WORK OF THE HOLY SPIRIT

SCRIPTURE:
The King James Version
John 16:5-15

16 **(5) But now I go MY way to HIM that sent ME; and none of you ask ME, whither goest THOU? (6) But because I have said these things unto you, sorrow hath filled your heart. (7) Nevertheless I tell you the truth; it is expedient for you that I go away: for if I go not away, the COMFORTER will not come unto you; but if I depart, I will send HIM unto you. (8) And when HE is come, HE will reprove the world of sin, and of righteousness, and of judgment: (9) Of sin, because they believe not on ME; (10) Of righteousness, because I go to MY FATHER, and ye see ME no more; (11) Of judgment, because the prince of this world is judged. (12) I have yet many things to say unto you, but ye cannot bear them now. (13) Howbeit when HE, the SPIRIT of TRUTH, is come, HE will guide you into all truth: for HE shall not speak of HIMSELF; but whatsoever HE shall hear, that shall HE speak: and HE will shew you things to come. (14) HE shall glorify ME: for HE shall receive of MINE, and shall shew it unto you. (15) All things that the FATHER hath are MINE: therefore said I, that HE shall take of MINE, and shall shew it unto you.**

COMMENTARY:

The departure of JESUS was necessary, no matter how painful it would be for HIS disciples. By now, they were so wrapped up in their own depression and problems, that, not even Thomas, cared to ask JESUS where it was that HE was going. They didn't quite realize at that time, just how beneficial JESUS' leaving would be for them, and, for the world at large. For without JESUS' death, burial, resurrection, and ascension, there could be no Gospel to preach and teach, nor, any atonement for sin. Furthermore, the HOLY SPIRIT could not be released into the lives of believers for all time, to help guide us, and comfort us, in our inevitable times of need.

The COMFORTER is the SPIRIT of GOD that was promised to us by the ancient prophets, and now, was being promised by JESUS HIMSELF. The HOLY SPIRIT came into the world, on the day of Pentecost, to "stay and abide" in those who believed on CHRIST, for all time. JESUS informed us that HIS ministry would consist of "reproving the world of sin, righteousness, and, judgment".

Sin in the world reached an all-time high with the crucifixion of our LORD and SAVIOR, JESUS CHRIST. And even today, our greatest sin continues to be our unbelief in HIM. When the world crucified JESUS, we, in effect, showed GOD that we thought HIS ONE and ONLY SON, was unrighteous. Righteousness was vindicated with the resurrection and ascension of CHRIST, and now the HOLY SPIRIT has come to convict us of our faulty views of JESUS, and, to inspire us to proclaim the truth of HIS Gospel to the same kind of world that slew HIM way back in the first century on Calvary Hill.

And finally, the HOLY SPIRIT's convicting work is concerned with judgment. The death and resurrection of JESUS CHRIST condemned satan, the prince of this world, to eternal damnation. People, who are rebelling against GOD, through sin, face the same defeat and judgment that satan has obtained. And just as JESUS brought glory to GOD, so too, will the HOLY SPIRIT bring glory to CHRIST JESUS.

SADNESS TURNED TO JOY
John 16:16-24

16 **(16)** "A little while, and ye shall not see ME: and again, a little while, and ye shall see ME, because I go to the FATHER." **(17)** Then said some of HIS disciples among themselves, "What is this that HE saith unto us, "A little while, and ye shall not see ME: and again, a little while, ye shall see ME:" and, "because I go to the FATHER?" **(18)** They said therefore, "What is this that HE saith, "A little while? We cannot tell what HE saith. **(19)** Now JESUS knew that they were desirous to ask HIM, and said unto them, "Do ye enquire among yourselves of that I said, A little while, and ye shall not see ME: and again, a little while, and ye shall see ME? **(20)** Verily, verily, I say unto you, That ye shall weep and lament, but the world shall rejoice: and ye shall be sorrowful, but your sorrow shall be turned into joy. **(21)** A woman when she is in travail hath sorrow, because her hour is come: but as soon as she is delivered of the child, she remembereth no more the anguish, for joy that a man is born into the world. **(22)** And ye now therefore have sorrow: but I will see you again, and your heart shall rejoice, and your joy no man taketh from you. **(23)** And in that day ye shall ask ME nothing. Verily, verily, I say unto you, Whatsoever ye shall ask the FATHER in MY name, HE will give it to you. **(24)** Hitherto have ye asked nothing in MY name: ask and ye shall receive, that your joy may be full.

COMMENTARY:

JESUS' private teachings now shift from the subject of the HOLY SPIRIT and HIS future work, to what the immediate future held for each of HIS disciples. John 16:16-24 deals mostly with the emotions of HIS disciples. At this point they were in deep sorrow and were also confused about some of JESUS' sayings. They were also afraid and really, by and large, were not having a very good night.

The phrase, "in a little while", that is used by JESUS in this passage was very confusing to this, now depressed, group of men. They wondered among themselves just what JESUS meant by the parables HE was uttering. They didn't realize at the time that JESUS was speaking of returning immediately after HIS crucifixion to minister to them, periodically, for an additional forty days before HIS ascension back into Heaven. However, JESUS did not clarify what HE meant, but chose instead, to let them come to understand what HE meant, in the process of time.

GOD brings joy to our lives, not by substituting our trials and pains, but rather, by our transformation and growth, from them. In John 16:21, JESUS gives just such an analogy to HIS disciples, as HE tries to reassure them that their sorrow, brought on by the news of HIM leaving, would soon be turned to joy over HIS return.

Here HE likens their woeful situation to that of a woman experiencing labor pains. At first, she suffers with excruciating pain, and then, after birth is given, all of her pain and anguish soon turns into joy because she has brought a new life into the world. With Christian joy, the pain that went before it, is soon forgotten, and the new feeling of that experience of joy, can never be taken away.

DIRECT ACCESS
John 16:25-33

16 **(25)** These things have I spoken unto you in proverbs, but I shall shew you plainly of the FATHER. **(26)** At that day ye shall ask in MY name: and I say not unto you, that I will pray the FATHER for you: **(27)** For the FATHER HIMSELF loveth you, because ye loved ME, and have believed that I came out from GOD. **(28)** I came forth from the FATHER, and AM come into the world: again, I leave the world, and go to the FATHER." **(29)** HIS disciples said unto HIM, "Lo, now speakest THOU plainly, and speakest no proverb, **(30)** Now are we sure that THOU knowest all things, and needest not that any man should ask THEE: by this we believe that THOU comest forth from GOD." **(31)** JESUS answered them, "Do ye now believe? (32) Behold, the hour cometh, yea, is now come, that ye shall be scattered, every man to his own, and shall leave ME alone: and yet I AM not alone, because the FATHER is with ME. (33) These things I have spoken unto you, that in ME ye might have peace. In the world ye shall have tribulation: but be of good cheer; I have overcome the world."

COMMENTARY:

In the New Testament Greek, the word used for "proverbs" is "paroimia" (paroy- mee-ah), and it is "an enigmatic, fictitious, illustration of what real life is all about". Its meaning is veiled to the casual listener, and it requires deep thought before its meaning becomes clear.

Up until this point, JESUS had been speaking to HIS disciples in "proverbs", or "parables", but HE promises them that, in time, it will not be necessary to do this, and HE will then, begin to speak to them plainly about GOD the FATHER. At that time they will be able to ask directly, anything of GOD, in JESUS' name, and GOD will grant it. It will no longer be necessary for JESUS to intercede personally on their behalf, because, after HIS death and resurrection, JESUS would serve as their permanent spiritual connection, directly to GOD in Heaven, whenever they wanted to communicate with HIM. All anyone has to do is believe on JESUS, and know that HE came from GOD, and GOD will bless you with abundant joy, and fill the desires of your heart.

When the disciples finally believed, they begin to understand exactly what JESUS was saying. A strange light seemed to come on, first in their hearts, and then their minds seemed to open up to receive the Word of GOD. The veil of truth had finally been lifted. However, JESUS cautioned them of the trials and tribulations that would soon scatter them away from HIM, leaving HIM only with the FATHER.

HE was telling them this ahead of time, so that when it happens, they will be able to regroup and find ultimate peace in HIM. Then, and only then, would they be able to find the strength they will need, in order to carry their own cross, and fight the battle with satan, that would ultimately come, and continue, throughout the remainder of their lives here on earth. And they would be able to take heart in the example that JESUS HIMSELF would set, as HE would soon complete HIS mission, by overcoming the gravitational pull of this world.

WHAT DID WE LEARN FROM CHAPTER SIXTEEN?
Here are some key points to remember

(1). The, HOLY SPIRIT was sent to us, by CHRIST JESUS. (John 16:7)

(2). The HOLY SPIRIT came to convince the world of its sin. (John 16:8-9)

(3). The HOLY SPIRIT came to convict us of our faulty views of JESUS, and to prove HIS righteousness to the world. (John 16:8 & 10)

(4). The HOLY SPIRIT came to convince the world of GOD's judgment against evil. (John 16:8 & 11)

(5). The HOLY SPIRIT came to guide us into all truth about CHRIST, and to glorify JESUS, just as JESUS glorifies GOD the FATHER. (John 16:13-15)

(6). GOD brings joy to our lives, not by substituting our trials and pains, but rather, by our transformation and growth, as a result of those experiences. (John 16:20-22)

(7). JESUS' sacrificial death and resurrection gives us direct access to GOD, when we pray and ask for anything in HIS name. (John 16:23-27)

CHAPTER SEVENTEEN:

JESUS' HIGH PRIESTLY PRAYER
(Prayer for HIMSELF)

SCRIPTURE:
King James Version
John 17:1-5

17 (1) These words spake JESUS, and lifted up HIS eyes to Heaven, and said, "FATHER, the hour is come; glorify THY SON, that THY SON also may glorify THEE: (2) As THOU hast given HIM power over all flesh, that HE should give eternal life to as many as THOU hast given HIM. (3) And this is life eternal, that they might know THEE the only true GOD, and JESUS CHRIST, WHOM THOU hast sent. (4) I have glorified THEE on the earth: I have finished the work which THOU gavest ME to do. (5) And now, O FATHER, glorify THOU ME with THINE OWN SELF with the glory which I had with THEE before the world was."

COMMENTARY:

After JESUS had ended HIS private teachings to HIS disciples in the Upper Room, HE left them with the profound statement, that, "HE had overcome the world". HE then looked up toward Heaven and began to pray, perhaps, the greatest prayer that has ever been prayed here on earth. It is the prayer of an over-comer, and JESUS is certainly the greatest over-comer of all times.

Here in John 17, verses 1-5, JESUS begins this prayer by praying for HIMSELF, however, in doing so, HE is also praying for us. As GOD's greatest servant, JESUS had every right to pray for the help HE needed from GOD in order to glorify HIS name. HIS request for glorification includes;

- Sustaining HIMSELF in HIS upcoming suffering,
- Acceptance of HIS vicarious sacrifice,
- Raising HIM up again, and then,
- Restoring HIM to HIS pre-incarnate glory.

HE had finished all of HIS other divine work, and now HE was ready to take on HIS final assignment so that HE could return back home to HIS FATHER WHO sent HIM.

We, as Christians, now know and understand that, for JESUS, the only way back to glory was through the cross, and so it must be, for those of us, who follow HIM. With open eyes, JESUS accepted the circumstances of the cross, so that whosoever believes in HIM, from that day forward, would not perish, but rather, would have everlasting life with our FATHER in Heaven.

When JESUS speaks of HIS actions bringing glory to GOD, HE is referring to the majesty and loveliness of GOD the FATHER that has been manifested through, what HE HIMSELF has done, and will do, in obedience to the FATHER. And after the FATHER has resurrected HIM from the dead, that act will also reflect the true majesty of HE HIMSELF, as the GOD-appointed SAVIOR of all of mankind.

This also lets man know that, when we obediently perform GOD's will, GOD will joyfully express HIMSELF through us also. And so we see here quite clearly, that, even we can display the same beauty and majesty that CHRIST JESUS displayed for the FATHER, when we pray for the strength to be able to perform our appointed duties for the LORD, here on earth, in this life.

JESUS' INTERCESSION FOR THE APOSTLES
John 17:6-19

17 (6) "I have manifested THY name unto the men which THOU gavest ME out of the world: THINE they were, and THOU gavest them to ME; and they have kept THY word. (7) Now they have known that all things whatsoever THOU hast given ME are of THEE. (8) For I have given unto them the words which THOU gavest ME; and they have received them, and have known surely that I came out from THEE, and they have believed that THOU didst send ME. (9) I pray for them: I pray not for the world, but for them which THOU hast given ME; for they are THINE. (10) And all MINE are THINE, and THINE are MINE; and I AM glorified in them. (11) And now I AM no more in the world, but these are in the world, and I come to THEE. HOLY FATHER, keep through THINE OWN name those whom THOU hast given ME, that they may be one, as WE are. (12) While I was with them in the world, I kept them in THY name: those that THOU gavest ME I have kept, and none of them is lost, but the son of perdition; that the scripture might be fulfilled. (13) And now come I to THEE; and these things I speak in the world, that they might have MY joy fulfilled in themselves. (14) I have given them THY word; and the world hath hated them, because they are not of the world, even as I AM not of the world. (15) I pray not that THOU shouldest take them out of the world, but that THOU shouldest keep them from evil. (16) They are not of the world, even as I AM not of the world. (17) Sanctify them through THY truth: THY word is truth. (18) As THOU hast sent ME into the world, even so have I also sent them into the world. (19) And for their sakes I sanctify MYSELF, that they also might be sanctified through the truth."

COMMENTARY:

JESUS' disciples obeyed the Word of GOD and HE praises them for it here in HIS prayer to the FATHER. JESUS loved them all the more for their avid, positive response to GOD's Word. HE had prayed for them, even before HE chose them, and now, this final prayer of intercession clearly reveals HIS loving concern for their continued well-being, after HIS departure back into Heaven.

These disciples were HIS original flock, given to HIM by GOD the FATHER, and HE had taken good care of them, during their three years together. HE had also been successful in taking them out of the world, and into a spiritual place, where HE HIMSELF had always dwelled. And while they were not perfect, they were all committed, (except Judas Iscariot) and passionately devoted to JESUS. They now, all believed in JESUS' oneness with the FATHER, and their faith was clearly manifested in their obedience to HIS teachings.

This section of the prayer focuses not only on the safety of the disciples, but also on the safety of all believers, who have chosen to come out of the world and into the realm where JESUS lives. Our safety has always, and, will forever depend on the nature of GOD, and not on our own conduct, or character. When JESUS was with HIS disciples physically, HE always kept them safe, and, they could always depend on HIS presence in their time of need. HE guided them then, the way the HOLY SPIRIT now guides us, and we, in addition, can still rest assure that JESUS is, even now, still praying for us from HIS Heavenly vantage point.

We don't ever need to walk around feeling sad and beaten down by the rigors of this world. We can, instead, be filled with joy, because our LORD and SAVIOR JESUS CHRIST has overcome the world, and HE is taking everyone with HIM, in victory, who chooses to come and share in HIS Kingdom.

JESUS' INTERCESSION FOR FUTURE BELIEVERS
John 17:20-26

17 (20) "Neither pray I for these alone, but for them also who shall believe on

ME through their word; (21) That they all may be one; as THOU, FATHER, art in ME, and I in THEE, that they also may be one in US: that the world may believe that THOU hast sent ME. (22) And the glory which THOU gavest ME I have given them: that they may be one, even as WE are one: (23) I in them, and THOU in ME, that they may be made perfect in one; and that the world may know that THOU hast sent ME, and hast loved them, as THOU hast loved ME. (24) FATHER, I will that they also, whom THOU hast given ME, be with ME where I AM; that they may behold MY glory, which THOU hast given ME: for THOU lovedst ME before the foundation of the world. (25) O righteous FATHER, the world hath not known THEE: but I have known THEE, and these have known that THOU hast sent ME. (26) And I have declared unto them THY name, and will declare it: that the love wherewith THOU hast loved ME may be in them, and I in them."

COMMENTARY:

This final segment of JESUS' prayer is for future believers who will choose to come to HIM through the teaching of HIS Word. In this, the "Church Age", every converted Christian came to be that way directly because of the work and witness of JESUS' original disciples. We see, all through this prayer, how JESUS goes out to the ends of the earth to save our otherwise, lost souls from the pits of hell.

First HE started with HIMSELF. Then HE moved on with HIS petition for HIS disciple's safety, and now, in the final section of this great petition, we see JESUS praying for the unity of all Christians, for all times, no matter where in the world they reside. And just as each high priest of Israel bore the names of the twelve tribes in GOD's presence in the tabernacle, so now does JESUS, in the Church Age, as the GREAT HIGH PRIEST, carry the names of all present and future believers into the glorious presence of the ALMIGHTY GOD in Heaven.

JESUS' request is a request for a "Christian unity" that will transcend all the differences that can be found among the Christian Church, as a whole. And even though we may never organize our Christian Churches in the same way, and we may never worship GOD in the same way, JESUS prayed that Christian Unity would forever transcend all these differences, and bring men together in fellowship and love.

The kind of unity that JESUS is praying for here in John 17 is also the kind of unity that the apostle Paul would later write about to the Churches, in all of his doctrinal letters. It is a unity, not born of bricks and mortar, but rather, it is a unity of "personal relationships", not unlike the one that we've already seen between the FATHER and the SON, which serves as an example to us to follow, for all time.

All believers belong to one body in CHRIST, and our spiritual unity is to be clearly shown through our behavior, or, the way we live. The spiritual unity of the FATHER and the SON is to be patterned in the Church. Without union with CHRIST JESUS, the Christian Church can do nothing in itself. "Christianity" is the only true religion, because, "Christianity" is the only religion that is a product of GOD's mind. The disciples' union with CHRIST resulted in the whole Christian community's belief in GOD the FATHER. The glory of the Church was born at the cross, but the unity in the Church was born before that, and it is personified in the spirit of JESUS and HIS original disciples.

All in all, we see four petitions for believers being included in this magnificent prayer. They are;

- "Preservation" (John 17:11)
- "Sanctification" (John 17:17)
- "Unity" (John 17:11, 21-22)
- "Participation" (John 17:24)

After JESUS prayed this prayer, HE would speak no more to HIS disciple, until after HIS "Passion" and Resurrection. And so we see HIS last words to HIS faithful, were not words of HIS despair, but rather, they were words concerning HIS "Glory".

WHAT DID WE LEARN FROM CHAPTER SEVENTEEN?
Here are some key points to remember

(1). We bring glory to GOD when we are obedient to HIS word. (John 17:4)

(2). JESUS existed, with GOD, before the world began. (John 17:5)

(3). In JESUS' "High Priestly Prayer", HE prayed first for HIMSELF.
(John 17:1-5)

(4). In JESUS' "High Priestly Prayer", HE prayed for HIS disciples.
(John 17:6-19)

(5). In JESUS' "High Priestly Prayer", HE prayed for all future believers.
(John 17:20-26)

(6). In JESUS' "High Priestly Prayer", HE prayed for "Christian Unity".

(John 17:11, & 21-26)

(7). JESUS prayed for Preservation (v.11), Sanctification (v.17),
Unity (v.11, 21-26), and Participation (v.24) of Christians.

CHAPTER EIGHTEEN:

JESUS' BETRAYAL AND ARREST

SCRIPTURE:
The King James Version
John 18:1-14

18 **(1)** When JESUS had spoken these words, HE went forth with HIS disciples over the brook Cedron, where was a garden, into the which HE entered, and HIS disciples. **(2)** And Judas also, which betrayed HIM, knew the place: for JESUS oft-times resorted thither with HIS disciples. **(3)** Judas then, having received a band of men and officers from the chief priests and Pharisees, cometh thither with lanterns and torches and weapons. **(4)** JESUS therefore, knowing all things that should come upon HIM, went forth, and said unto them, "Whom seek ye? **(5)** They answered HIM, "JESUS of Nazareth". JESUS said unto them, "I AM HE". And Judas also, which betrayed HIM, stood with them. **(6)** As soon then as HE had said unto them, "I AM HE", they went backward, and fell to the ground. **(7)** Then asked HE them again, "Whom seek ye?" And they said, "JESUS of Nazareth". **(8)** JESUS answered, "I have told you that I AM HE: if therefore ye seek ME, let these go their way:" **(9)** That the saying might be fulfilled, which HE spake, "Of them which THOU gavest ME have I lost none". **(10)** Then Simon Peter having a sword drew it, and smote the high priest's servant, and cut off his right ear. The servant's name was Malchus. **(11)** Then said JESUS unto Peter, "Put up thy sword into the sheath: the cup which MY FATHER hath given ME, shall I not drink it? **(12)** Then the band and the captain and officers of the Jews took JESUS, and bound HIM, **(13)** And led HIM away to Annas first; for he was father in law to Caiaphas, which was the high priest that same year. **(14)** Now Caiaphas was he, which gave counsel to the Jews, that it was expedient that one man should die for the people.

COMMENTARY:

After JESUS finished praying, HE and HIS disciples crossed the "Kidron Valley" to the east. The Kidron Valley, now the "Wodi en-NAR", is a valley, which begins north of Jerusalem and passes between the temple mount and the Mount of Olives, and then ends at the Dead Sea. Ironically, it is the same place where David learned that he had been betrayed by his trusted friend, Ahithophel and his son Absalom, some 950 years earlier (2 Samuel 15:23. 30-31). And now, as it turns out, it would be this same site where Judas Iscariot was about to betray JESUS, on this, the eve of HIS crucifixion.

The Olive grove was a place where JESUS often came with HIS disciples whenever they were in Jerusalem, and so, it was a place that Judas Iscariot was also very familiar with. He knew exactly where to lead the band of Roman soldiers, who were dispersed there by the religious leaders to arrest JESUS, and put HIM on trial. Judas had already sold JESUS out to them for thirty pieces of silver (the price of a common slave), and now he was there to complete his deal with the Pharisees, by betraying his MASTER's love for him, with a kiss.

As the battalion of 600 soldiers arrived at the olive garden of Gethsemane with torches blazing, lanterns glowing, and weapons drawn, JESUS fully realized what was taking place. Stepping forward HE asked them anyway, who was it that they were seeking? The mob replied "JESUS of Nazareth" and JESUS responded that, "I AM HE".

When HE said these words, every single one of the men in the battalion fell backwards to the ground. Perhaps what we see here is a manifestation of JESUS' divine power and majesty, or, it could have also been a fulfillment of the statement of David in Psalm 27:2-3. However, it is more likely that we see here, is both of those scenarios being played out. JESUS then suggests to the soldiers that they take HIM, and leave HIS disciples alone. HE was willing to protect them by giving over HIS OWN life instead of the lives of HIS friends.

And even after Simon Peter draws his sword and cuts off the ear of Malchus, one of the servants of the high priest who had come with the soldier to take JESUS, JESUS still rebukes HIS disciple and commands HIM to put up his sword. And then, in the true sense of the statement, "Love your enemy", another gospel account (Luke) tells us that JESUS picked up the ear of Malchus, and miraculously restored it to his head. At this point JESUS was ready to go forward to HIS "Passion", and was determined to drink the cup, that HIS beloved FATHER, had already set before HIM.

PETER'S DENIALS
John 18:15-27

18 15) And Simon Peter followed JESUS, and so did another disciple: that disciple was known unto the high priest, and went with JESUS into the palace of the high priest. (16) But Peter stood at the door without. Then went out that other disciple, which was known unto the high priest, and spake unto her that kept the door, and brought in Peter. (17) Then saith the damsel that kept the door unto Peter, "Art thou also one of this MAN's disciples? He saith, "I am not". (18) And the servants and officers stood there, who had made a fire of coals; for it was cold: and they warmed themselves: and Peter stood with them, and warmed himself. (19) The high priest then asked JESUS of HIS disciples, and of HIS doctrine. (20) JESUS answered him, "I spake openly to the world; I ever taught in the synagogue, and in the temple, whither the Jews always resort; and in secret have I said nothing. (21) Why askest thou ME? Ask them which heard ME, what I have said unto them: behold, they know what I said." (22) And when HE had thus spoken, one of the officers which stood by struck JESUS with the palm of his hand, saying, "Answerest THOU the high priest so?" (23) JESUS answered him, "If I have spoken evil, bear witness of the evil: but if well, why smitest thou ME?" (24) Now Annas had sent HIM bound unto Caiaphas the high priest. (25) And Simon Peter stood and warmed himself. They said therefore unto him, "Art not thou also one of HIS disciples?" He denied it, and said, "I am not". (26) One of the servants of the high priest, being his kinsman whose ear Peter cut off, saith, "Did not I see thee in the garden with HIM?" (27) Peter then denied again: and immediately the cock crew.

COMMENTARY:

After JESUS allowed the soldiers to arrest HIM, Peter and one of the other disciples followed them back into the city. The unnamed disciple here, was known by the high priest, and thereby, had access to the high priest's courtyard. He was also able to gain permission for Peter's entrance into the courtyard, from the lady who kept the door. However, the lady recognized Peter as one of JESUS' disciples, and when she inquired this of him, for the first time, he denied that he knew JESUS.

Here we see a very human, but somewhat complicated side of Peter. Only moments earlier he had been this brave, defiant defender of JESUS, while in the garden of Gethsemane. Now, we see him cowering down under the pressure of the reality of what courage a man has to have in order to follow in the footsteps of CHRIST.

Throughout the history of the Church, Christians have often faced martyrdom bravely, but there are perhaps even more times when they buckled under at the threat of death. Ironically, the other disciple didn't seem to have a problem with being known as a follower of CHRIST. He was well known by the lady at the door, and the high priest, yet, he did not try to hide, or play the role of a secret Christian, but rather, he entered boldly into the temple to be near JESUS.

Peter went on in and stood at the fire with the guards and household servants, and began to warm himself as the high priest, Annas, begin his questioning of JESUS. He was now gripped with fear and perhaps, having second thoughts as to why he came there in the first place. This questioning of JESUS, by Annas, was one of three religious trials, and was the first of the six total trials that JESUS would endure on that night before HIS crucifixion.

Annas, according to record, was high priest from A.D. 6 to A.D. 15. He was then deposed by the Romans, but managed to keep control of the post through his four sons, and his son-in-law Caiaphas for a number of years after his disposal. Caiaphas, was the official high priest from A.D. 18 to A.D. 36, which covered the time period of JESUS' public ministry. However, we see the power still wielded by Annas, in that JESUS was brought to him first.

Annas begins his questioning of JESUS by asking HIM about HIS followers and what HE had been teaching them. JESUS responds to the question by defending the transparency of HIS doctrine, which HE had been teaching openly in the temple and synagogues for three years. One of the temple guards, who did not like the way JESUS answered, struck JESUS in the face. After this, Annas sent JESUS over to see Caiaphas for further questioning.

In the meantime, Peter, who was still standing by the fire, was asked again, if he was one of JESUS' disciples, and again, he denied that he was. Then, one of the household servants, who was a relative of Malchus, the man whose ear was cut off by Peter in the olive garden, thought he recognized Peter as one of JESUS' followers. But when he asked the frightened disciple if this was true, for the third and final time, Peter denied even knowing JESUS. And then immediately, true to JESUS' words, Peter heard the prophetic sound of the rooster's crow.

THE CIVIL TRIAL BEFORE PILATE
John 18:28-40

18 (28) Then led they JESUS from Caiaphas unto the hall of judgment: and it was early; and they themselves went not into the judgment hall, lest they should be defiled; but that they might eat Passover. (29) Pilate then went out unto them, and said, "What accusation bring ye against this MAN?" (30) They answered and said unto him, "If HE were not a malefactor, we would not have delivered HIM up unto thee." (31) Then said Pilate unto them, "Take ye HIM, and judge HIM according to your law". The Jews therefore said unto him, "It is

not lawful for us to put any man to death:”
(32) That the saying of JESUS might be fulfilled, which HE spake, signifying what death HE should die. (33) Then Pilate entered into the judgment hall again, and called JESUS, and said unto HIM, “Art THOU the King of the Jews?” (34) JESUS answered him, “Sayest thou this thing of thyself, or did others tell it thee of ME?” (35) Pilate answered, “Am I a Jew? THINE OWN nation and the chief priests have delivered THEE unto me: what hast THOU done?” (36) JESUS answered, “MY kingdom is not of this world: if MY kingdom were of this world, then would MY servants fight, that I should not be delivered to the Jews: but now is MY kingdom not from hence.” (37) Pilate therefore said unto HIM, “Art THOU a king then?” JESUS answered, “Thou sayest that I AM a king. To this end I was born, and for this cause came I into the world, that I should bear witness unto the truth. Every one that is of the truth heareth MY voice.” (38) Pilate saith unto HIM, “What is the truth?” And when he said this, he went out again unto the Jews, and saith unto them, “I find in HIM no fault at all.” (39) But ye have a custom that I should release unto you, one at the Passover: will ye therefore that I release unto you the KING of the Jews?” (40) Then cried they all again, saying, “Not this MAN, but Barabbas”. Now Barabbas was a robber.

COMMENTARY:

JESUS’ second religious trial, the, trial before Caiaphas, ended in the early morning hours of the day of JESUS’ crucifixion. HE was then taken to the headquarters of the Roman governor, Pontius Pilate. JESUS’ accusers, the Jewish religious leaders, did not enter into the governor’s headquarters, because they were “self-forbidden” from entering into the house of a Gentile, especially during Passover. So apparently they must have sent JESUS in alone, while they stood outside and awaited Pilate’s decision.

Pilate’s apparent wavering, during JESUS’ “first civil trial”, should not be mistaken for virtue. For a quick look at Pilate’s personal history with the Jews will show us how he used the path of least resistance, in order to save himself from his own, “self-imposed” troubled career.

When Pilate first entered into Jerusalem as Procurator, he got off to a very bad start with the Jews and their religious hierarchy by entering into the city wearing the “standards” of the Roman Emperor on their helmets. The Jews considered these standards to be idolatrous, because the Romans worshiped the Caesars as gods. Every Roman governor, before Pilate, had respected their wishes and removed these emblems from their headgear while they were in Jerusalem. Pilate, on the other hand, steadfastly refused to do so, despite being constantly dogged by the Jews.

Finally, in a showdown at the amphitheater in Jerusalem, Pilate surrounded a group of protesting Jews with armed soldiers and told them that if they didn't put an end to their requests, they would be killed right there on the spot. The Jews, however, called Pilate's bluff, forcing him to reconsider. They knew that Pilate would come under fire from the Emperor, Caesar Tiberius, if he found out what Pilate was trying to do. And so Pilate, to his own dismay, had to buckle under and admit defeat.

A second incident involved Pilate's taking of money from the temple treasury, in order to help finance a new aqueduct system for Jerusalem. When some of the angry Jews protested, Pilate planted some of his soldiers into the crowd, and upon his signal, they attacked the Jews, injuring many, and even killing some innocent bystanders.

It was these two incidents that the Jews used to blackmail Pilate into doing their desired will, of giving JESUS the death sentence. They knew, and Pilate knew, that if Tiberius found out about either one of these incidences, Pilate would be driven from office, or perhaps, even killed by his Roman superiors.

One might ask himself, "Why didn't the Jews just take JESUS out and kill HIM themselves?" Well, the truth is that, about forty years before the destruction of the temple by the Romans, Emperor Julius Caesar took away the right of the Jews to make decisions of judgment that involved the life and death of its citizens. Since that time, only the Roman government could give a person a death sentence and carry it out (John 18:31).

In addition, it was important to the Jewish religious hierarchy that JESUS, die, by Roman method, "hanging from a cross", and here's why. According to Deuteronomy 21:22-23, anyone who has committed a crime worthy of death, and is executed and hung on a tree, it is an indication that that person was cursed of GOD. And so, not only did the religious leaders want to convince the people that JESUS was "not the SON of GOD", as HE had claimed, they also wanted to send a message that HE was even "cursed of GOD". However, ironically, from a GODly perspective, this manner of death would be in line with the prophetic statement of JESUS, where HE says, "When HE is raised up, HE will draw all men to HIM".

After Pilate's questioning of JESUS had ended, he once again went out to the people and declared that "he could find no fault in JESUS". He even tried to compromise the truth of his finding, by offering to release JESUS as result of their customary rule, where they would release one prisoner from custody each year at the Passover. But instead of using that opportunity to free JESUS from custody, the Jewish people chose instead, to release a convicted robber by the name of Barabbas.

WHAT DID WE LEARN FROM CHAPTER EIGHTEEN?
Here are some key points to remember

(1). JESUS" betrayal by Judas Iscariot took place in the same area (the Kidron Valley) where David was when he was betrayed by Ahithophel and Absolom. (John 18:1)

(2). JESUS let HIMSELF get arrested in accordance with GOD's will, and HE showed HIS power over the regimen of 600 men by knocking them all to ground just by speaking three words "I AM HE". (John 18:6)

(3). JESUS was first tried, by Annas, the former high priest. It was also JESUS' first, of three religious trials, that are recorded in the four gospels (John 18:19-24)

(4). Peter denied knowing JESUS three times, just as JESUS had predicted to him earlier. (John 18:17 & 25-27)

(5). JESUS' trial before Pilate is HIS fourth trial overall, that is recorded the four gospel accounts. It is also HIS first, of three civil trials. (John 18:40)

(6). Only the Romans had the power to execute a human being. (John 18:31)

(7). The Jews chose Barabbas, a convicted criminal, over JESUS. (John 18:39-40)

CHAPTER NINETEEN:

(115)

JESUS SENTENCED TO DEATH

SCRIPTURE:
The King James Version
John 19:1-16

19 (1) Then Pilate therefore took JESUS, and scourged HIM. (2) And the soldiers platted a crown of thorns, and put it on HIS head, and they put on HIM a purple robe, (3) And said, "Hail. King of the Jews! And they smote HIM with their hands. (4) Pilate therefore went forth again, and saith unto them, "Behold, I bring HIM forth to you, that ye may know that I find no fault in HIM". (5) Then came Jesus forth, wearing the crown of thorns, and the purple robe. And Pilate saith unto them, "Behold the MAN!". (6) When the chief priests therefore and officers saw HIM, they cried out, saying, "Crucify HIM, crucify HIM". Pilate saith unto them, "Take ye HIM, and crucify HIM: for I find no fault in HIM". (7) The Jews answered him, "We have a law, and by our law HE ought to die, because HE made HIMSELF the SON of GOD". (8) When Pilate therefore heard that saying, he was the more afraid; (9) And went again into the judgment hall, and saith unto JESUS, Whence art THOU? But JESUS gave no answer. (10) Then saith Pilate unto HIM, "Speakest THOU not unto me? Knowest THOU not that I have power to crucify THEE, and have power to release THEE? (11) JESUS answered, "Thou couldest have no power at all against ME. Except it were given thee from above: therefore he that delivered ME unto thee hath the greater sin". (12) And from thenceforth Pilate sought to release HIM: but the Jews cried out saying, "If thou let this man go, thou art not Caesar's friend: whosoever maketh himself a king speaketh against Caesar". (13) When Pilate therefore heard that saying, he brought JESUS forth, and sat down in the judgment seat in a place that is called the Pavement, but in Hebrew, Gabbatha. (14) And it was the preparation of the Passover, and about the sixth hour: and he saith unto the Jews, "Behold your king!" (15) But they cried out, "Away with HIM, away with HIM, crucify HIM". Pilate saith unto them, "Shall I crucify your KING?" The chief priests answered, "We have no king but Caesar". (16) Then delivered he HIM therefore unto them to be crucified. And they took JESUS, and led HIM away.

COMMENTARY:

To compromise the truth, is to not stand behind the truth at all. We either hold fast to the things of GOD, or, we allow ourselves to be deceived by satan, just as when we doubt GOD's goodness, we automatically become attracted to satan's offers.

The Jews delivered JESUS into the hands of Pilate, and despite his finding JESUS innocent, Pilate tried to compromise the truth of his findings (John 18:38-39 & 19:7)). He convinced himself in the end that he had done all that he could, but actually, he knew even deeper in his heart that he had long ago, through his problems with the Jews, tossed away his option to do the right thing. Through his earlier actions against the Jews, he had already set himself up to be blackmailed by the Jewish hierarchy in Jerusalem.

The "permissive will" of GOD, allows for man to do many things, and ultimately, through JESUS' death, we also receive GOD's wonderful and abounding grace. However, GOD, through HIS infinite wisdom, will never allow "grace" to trump "truth". The "TRUTH" presented itself to Pilate that day, in the person of JESUS CHRIST, and he decided to put TRUTH to death. And, as for as the Jews were concerned, in order to carry out the death of JESUS, they were willing to abandon every principle that they ever had, especially on this day, when they uttered these infamous words to Pilate, as it is recorded in John 19:15, where they state, "We have no king but Caesar". It was a final abandonment of the GOD that they had always preached that they served.

That also put the final brush strokes on a tragic painting, of a maddened mob, that had been driven by anger. Driven by their hatred for JESUS, the Jews lost all sense of proportion, and they totally forgot about the mercy, they themselves, had so often preached about in the temple. They forgot all justice, and, in the end, they denounced GOD, and professed Caesar. Never before, in the history of man, has hatred's insanity presented itself before us this vividly, and hopefully, it never will again.

There can never be a "right time" to do the "wrong thing", as Pilate and the Jews ultimately did on that day. They took the most beautiful LIFE, that ever did live, and then, they snuffed it out, on a cross.

THE CRUCIFIXION, DEATH, AND BURIAL OF JESUS
John 19:17-42

19 **(17)** And HE bearing HIS cross went forth into a place called the place of a skull, which is called in Hebrew Golgotha: **(18)** Where they crucified HIM, and two other with HIM, on either side one, and JESUS in the midst. **(19)** And Pilate wrote a title, and put it on the cross. And the writing was, "JESUS of Nazareth the King of the Jews". **(20)** This title then read many of the Jews: for the place where JESUS was crucified was nigh to the city: and it was written in Hebrew, and Greek, and Latin. **(21)** Then said the chief priests of the Jews to Pilate, "Write not, "The King of the Jews": but that HE said, "I AM king of the Jews". **(22)** Pilate answered, "What I have written I have written. **(23)** Then the soldiers, when they had crucified JESUS, took HIS garments, and made four parts, to every soldier a part; and also HIS coat: now the coat was without seam, woven from the top throughout. **(24)** They said therefore among themselves, "Let us not rend it, but cast lots for it, whose it shall be; that the scripture might be fulfilled, which saith, "They parted MY raiment among them, and for MY vesture they did cast lots". These things therefore the soldiers did. **(25)** Now there stood by the cross of JESUS HIS mother, and HIS mother's sister, Mary the wife of Cleophas, and Mary Magdelene. **(26)** When JESUS therefore saw HIS mother, and the disciple standing by, whom HE loved, HE saith unto HIS mother, "Woman, behold thy son!" **(27)** Then saith HE to the disciple, "Behold thy mother!" And from that hour that disciple took her unto his own home. **(28)** After this, JESUS knowing that all things were now accomplished, that the scripture might be fulfilled, saith, "I thirst". **(29)** Now there was a set of a vessel full of vinegar: and they filled a spunge with vinegar, and put it upon hyssop, and put it to HIS mouth. **(30)** When JESUS therefore had received the vinegar, HE said, "It is finished:" and HE bowed HIS head, and gave up the GHOST. **(31)** The Jews therefore, because it was the preparation, that the bodies should not remain upon the cross on the Sabbath day, (for that Sabbath day was an high day,) besought Pilate that their legs might be broken, and that they might be taken away. **(32)** Then came the soldiers, and brake the legs of the first, and of the other which was crucified with him. **(33)** But when they came to JESUS, and saw that HE was dead already, they brake not HIS legs: **(34)** But one of the soldiers with a spear pierced HIS side, and forthwith came there out blood and water. **(35)** And he that saw it bare record, and his record is true: and he knoweth that he saith true, that ye might believe. **(36)** For these things were done, that the scripture should be fulfilled, "A bone of HIM shall not be broken". **(37)** And again another scripture saith, "They shall look on HIM

WHOM they pierced". (38) And after this Joseph of Arimathaea, being a disciple of JESUS, but secretly for fear of the Jews, besought Pilate that he might take away the body of JESUS: and Pilate gave him leave. He came therefore, and took the body of JESUS (39) And there came also Nicodemus, which at the first came to JESUS by night, and brought a mixture of myrrh and aloes, about an hundred pound weight. (40) Then took they the body of JESUS, and wound it in linen clothes with spices, as the manner of the Jews is to bury. (41) Now in the place where HE was crucified there was a garden; and in the garden a new sepulcher, wherein was never a man yet laid, (42) There laid they JESUS therefore because of the Jews' preparation day; for the sepulcher was nigh at hand.

COMMENTARY:

In John 19:17-42, Matthew 27:32-50, Mark 15:21-37, and Luke 23:26-46, the authors all give their respective accounts of the "Crucifixion of CHRIST JESUS". John and Matthew were eyewitnesses. John Mark wrote of Peter's recollections, whom, himself, was an eyewitness, and Luke's account is, by his own admission, a result of careful investigative work, and interviewing of the early Disciples and eyewitnesses to JESUS' Ministry.

What follows, will be my attempt to incorporate these four accounts into one accurate depiction of this tragic and unjust event. All accounts begin with JESUS' death walk to Golgotha (Skull Hill), where HE is ultimately crucified by Roman method. However, Mark, Matthew, and Luke include in their accounts of how, on the way, JESUS and HIS executioners make a divine encounter with a man called Simon, who is compelled by a Roman soldier, to carry the cross of JESUS.

Here, we see, in Simon, a man who has come all the way from Cyrene, on the continent of Africa, to, no doubt, participate in the Passover Celebration, but instead, ends up becoming the first Gentile to perform a Christian mission. It is well worth noting that since that moment, no man has, or ever will again, be forced, to carry the cross of our LORD and SAVIOR, JESUS CHRIST. It must now and forever be a "voluntary act", if we are to choose to do the work of CHRIST.

As they walked along, great crowds of people, including many grief stricken women, followed them. But JESUS turned and said to them, "Daughters of Jerusalem, don't weep for me, but weep for yourselves, and for your children. For the days are coming when they will say, "Fortunate indeed are the women who are childless, the wombs that have not borne a child and the breasts that have never nursed. People will beg the mountains to fall on them, and the hills to bury them.

For if these things are done when the tree is green, what will happen when it is dry?" (Luke 23:28-31 - NLT).

When a criminal was condemned to be crucified, he was taken from the judgment hall and put in the middle of four Roman soldiers. His cross was then laid upon his shoulders, and he was marched to the place of crucifixion, by the longest possible route. In front of him marched another soldier holding a placard, or "sign" stating what the convicted person's crime was.

In JESUS' case, Pilate had the words, inscribed, "JESUS of Nazareth the King of the Jews", much to the dismay of the Jewish religious leaders. They had tried to get him to change it to "HE said" HE was the KING of the Jews". However, Pilate saw this as a last ditch attempt to fire back at the Jewish religious leaders for forcing his hand in this ordeal with JESUS' trial. So, not only did he refuse to change it, but he also had it written in three different languages, Aramaic, Latin, and Greek.

In Matthew 26:29, Mark 14:25, and Luke 22:18, JESUS promises HIS Disciples that HE will not drink wine again until HE drinks it new, with them in the Kingdom of GOD. In Psalms 69:21, the Psalmist tells us that JESUS would be offered sour wine to satisfy HIS thirst. We see Scripture being fulfilled in Matt. 27:34 & 48, Mark 15:23 & 36, Luke 23:36, & John 19:29-30, where JESUS is offered wine on two occasions and refused to drink. These can also be viewed as final attempts by Satan to trip JESUS up, on HIS promise, HE had made to HIS Disciples, during HIS establishment of the New Covenant, at the Last Supper.

We see further fulfillment of Scripture, with the Roman soldiers gambling, or "casting lots" for JESUS' clothing, (Matt. 27:35, Mark 15:24, Luke 23:34b, & John 19:23-24). This fulfills one of the seven prophesies found in Psalms 22, (22:18), which states, "They part my garments among them, and cast lots upon my vesture" (KJV).

There were two criminals, who were crucified with JESUS that day, one on each side of HIM. One, strangely enough, felt like he was in a position to mock JESUS. The other defended JESUS' innocence, and thereby, became the last person saved by JESUS, during HIS earthly ministry (Luke 23:39-43).

Standing near the cross that day, were Mary, JESUS' mother, her sister Mary, the wife of Cleophas (who is said to be the same as Alpheus, the father of James and Joseph), Zebedee's wife (the mother of James and John), Mary Magdalene, and the Apostle John. Looking down from the cross, and seeing HIS mother's anguish, JESUS consigns her care, into the hands of the Apostle John, the Disciple whom HE loved.

These words of JESUS to Mary and John, was the third of seven statements, or sayings, HE made from the cross, HE says to Mary "Woman, behold thy son", and to John, "Behold thy mother" (John 19:26-27). The other six statements can be found in the following verses: Matthew 27:46, Luke 23:34, 43 & 46, & John 19:28b & 30a.

At noon, darkness fell across the sky, and lasted until three o'clock. JESUS speaks HIS sixth utterance, "tetelestai" (tet-el-es-ahee), the Greek word for "it is finished", or "paid in full". HE then bows HIS head and utters HIS seventh and final saying, "FATHER, into THY hands I commend MY Spirit", and HE gave up the GHOST.

There is an ensuing Earthquake, and the curtains in the Temple were torn from top to bottom. Later, the Jews went to Pilate to request that the bodies of the three be removed before the Sabbath, and that their legs be broken to expedite death. Pilate granted the request and the legs of the two criminals hanging beside JESUS were broken. However, they saw that JESUS' body had already expired and they didn't break HIS legs.

One of the soldiers did, however, take a spear and pierce JESUS' body in the side to ensure that HE was dead. In John 19:34, the Apostle tells us that blood and water came from JESUS' wound after HE had been pierced with the spear. We know that normally, the body of a dead person will not bleed.

It is medically suggested that JESUS' experiences, physically and emotionally, leading up to HIS death, were so terrible, that HIS heart must have ruptured. When that happened, the blood of the heart mingled with the fluid of the Pericardium, which surrounds the heart. In all likelihood, the spear of the soldier pierced the Pericardium, causing the blood and water mixture to spew out. And so we see that, in the end, JESUS died, quite literally, from a broken heart.

This passage, by John, is final proof that JESUS was a real human with a real human body, bone of our bone, and flesh of our flesh. The water and blood, which flowed from JESUS' side, were, to John, and should be to all Christians, a sign of the cleansing water of baptism, and the cleansing blood commemorated, and experienced, in the LORD's Supper.

WHAT DID WE LEARN FROM CHAPTER NINETEEN?
Here are some key points to remember

(1). Despite feeling that JESUS was innocent, Pilate has JESUS flogged with a Lead tipped whip. (John 19:1)

(2). The Roman soldiers placed a crown of long, sharp thorns on JESUS' head, and then, wrapped HIM in a purple robe. (John 19:2)

(3). When the Jewish leaders saw JESUS, they began shouting, "Crucify HIM, Crucify HIM. (John 19:6)

(4). The Jewish leaders denounced GOD, and professed Caesar as their king. (John 19:15)

(5). The apostle John was given the assignment of taking care of JESUS' mother, after HIS death. (John 19:26-27)

(6). Joseph of Arimathea buried JESUS in a tomb that was originally purchased for himself. (John 19:38-42) (Luke 23:50-56) (Matthew 27:57-61) (Mark 15:42-46)

(7). Nicodemus assisted Joseph of Arimathea in JESUS' burial. (John 19:39-42)

CHAPTER TWENTY:

(122)

THE RESURRECTION OF CHRIST JESUS

SCRIPTURE:
The King James Version
John 20:1-18

20 **(1)** The first day of the week cometh Mary Magdalene early, when it was yet dark, unto the sepulcher, and seeth the stone taken away from the sepulcher. **(2)** Then she runneth, and cometh to Simon Peter, and to the other disciple, whom JESUS loved, and saith unto them, "They have taken away the LORD out of the sepulcher, and we know not where they have laid HIM". **(3)** Peter therefore went forth, and that other disciple, and came to the sepulcher. **(4)** So they ran both together: and the other disciple did outrun Peter, and came first to the sepulcher. **(5)** And he stooping down, and looking in, saw the linen clothes lying; yet went he not in. **(6)** Then cometh Simon Peter following him, and went into the sepulcher, and seeth the linen clothes lie, **(7)** And the napkin, that was about HIS head, not lying with the linen clothes, but wrapped together in a place by itself. **(8)** Then went in also that other disciple, which came first to the sepulcher, and he saw, and believed. **(9)** For as yet they knew not the scripture, that HE must rise again from the dead. **(10)** Then the disciples went away again unto their own home. **(11)** But Mary stood without at the sepulcher weeping: and as she wept, she stooped down, and looked into the sepulcher, **(12)** And seeth two angels in white sitting, the one at the head, and the other at the feet, were the body of JESUS had lain. **(13)** And they say unto her, "Woman, why weepest thou? She saith unto them, "Because they have taken away my LORD, and I know not where they have laid HIM. **(14)** And when she had thus said, she turned herself back, and saw JESUS standing, and knew not that it was JESUS. **(15)** JESUS saith unto her, "Woman, why weepest thou? Whom seekest thou?" She, supposing HIM to be the gardener, saith unto HIM, "SIR, if THOU have borne HIM hence, tell me where THOU hast laid HIM, and I will take HIM away. **(16)** JESUS saith unto her, "Mary". She turned herself, and saith unto HIM, "RABBONI"; which is to say, "MASTER". **(17)** JESUS saith unto her, "Touch ME not; for I AM not yet ascended to MY FATHER: but go to MY brethren, and say unto them, I ascend unto MY FATHER, and your FATHER; and to MY GOD, and your GOD." **(18)** Mary Magdalene came and told the disciples that she had seen the LORD, and that HE had spoken these things unto her.

COMMENTARY:

In the Greek, the word New Testament writers use for "resurrection" is "anastasis" (an-as-tas-is), and it is "a moral recovery of spiritual truth". It also means, in the physical sense, "to stand up again". In John chapter 20, verses 1-18, Matthew 28:1-10, Mark 16:1-19, and Luke 24:1-12, these authors of GOD share their respective Gospel accounts of the Resurrection of our LORD and SAVIOR, JESUS CHRIST.

The Resurrection of CHRIST is the essence of the Christian faith, and the core of all of the Apostles teachings. All accounts tell us that it was early in the morning of the first day of the week, while it was still dark, when JESUS' body was discovered missing. By combining all four Gospel accounts, we can see that Mary Magdalene, the woman from whom JESUS removed seven demons (Luke 8:2), Mary, the mother of James and Joseph, Salome, who was Zebedee's wife and the mother of James and John, and Joanna, the wife of Chuza, Herod's business manager, all went to the tomb of JESUS to anoint HIS body for burial, with spices.

Perhaps no one had ever loved JESUS as much as Mary Magdalene did. HE had done something for her that no one else could ever do, and she never forgot it. It was the custom of the Jews to visit the tomb of a loved one for three days after the body had been laid to rest. They believed that, for three days, the spirit of the deceased person would hover around the tomb, and only departed when the decomposing body became unrecognizable.

The day following JESUS' Crucifixion was the Sabbath, which is our Saturday, so to visit on that day would violate the Sabbath law. That is why their first visit had to occur on that early Sunday morning. The original Greek writings of the New Testament authors tell us that, it was during "proi" when they visited the tomb. The Jews divided their nights into four watches. The first night watch was from 6 p.m. to 9 p.m., the second watch was from 9 p.m. to 12 a.m., the third watch was from 12 a.m. to 3 a.m., and the fourth and final watch was from 3 a.m. to 6 a.m. It was during this forth watch, called "proi", that, the women came to the tomb.

Tombs, in those days, were "cave-like" compartments that had been carved into the side of a hill, or mountain, and then, covered by a circular shaped rock, which rested, in a slanted groove that had been carved out, along the front opening of these compartments. This extremely heavy rock had to be rolled uphill to open, and downhill to close. So we can envision that it was much harder to open than it was to close.

In addition, Matthew tells us that JESUS' tomb was also sealed by Roman officials, at the request of the Jewish leaders (Matthew 27:62-66). They also placed guards out in front of the tomb. Matthew also records that there was a great earthquake associated with an angel of the LORD, who came down from Heaven and rolled away the stone from the entrance of the sepulcher, and then, sat on it. This apparently frightened the Roman guards so much, that they actually fainted (Matthew 28:2-4).

When the women arrived at the tomb, they were shocked and frightened by what they saw. However, the angel was able to allay their fears and invite them to look into the cave, so they could see that JESUS was no longer there. He then urged them to go and tell JESUS' Disciples the good news, that, JESUS had arisen from the dead, just as HE had said that HE would.

The women then ran and found Peter and John, who were still somewhat puzzled, and were thinking someone had broken into the tomb and removed JESUS' body (John 20:2). Peter and John then ran to the tomb, and with John arriving first, he looks in and sees JESUS' body wrappings lying there in the tomb, however, he sees no body.

Peter then arrives and actually goes into the cave, where he too, only sees the cloth that had enwrapped JESUS' body. When Peter saw this, he remembered and realized what Scripture had said, and, what JESUS had said about rising from the dead after three days, and he believed, and they went home.

John tells us in 20:11-18, that afterwards, Mary Magdalene was standing outside the tomb weeping, and as she wept, she peered inside the cave. She saw two white-robed angels, sitting at the head and foot of where JESUS' body had lain. One of the angels asked her, why was she crying? Mary, still not understanding, replies, "Because they have taken away my LORD, and I don't know where they have put HIM".

Just then, she noticed someone standing behind her, that, she thought was the gardener (she didn't recognize, at that time, that it was JESUS, probably because her eyes were filled with tears). "Sir", she said, "If you have taken HIM away, tell me where you have put HIM". JESUS then speaks to her, and she apparently recognizes HIS voice and runs to hug HIM. However, JESUS tells her not to cling to HIM, because HE had not yet ascended to HIS FATHER. Mary then ran to find the Disciples once again, but this time, to tell them that she had actually seen the risen LORD.

We see throughout these "Passion Narratives" of the Bible, that this lady, Mary Magdalene, was always there, in the vicinity, of our LORD and SAVIOR. She was there at the foot of the cross, when JESUS' earthly life expired, on that infamous Friday in world history (John 19:25). She was there when JESUS' body was wrapped and entombed, by Joseph of Arimathea (Matthew 27:61, Mark 15:47) and Nicodemus (John 19:39-40).

And she was also there when the empty tomb was discovered, early that Sunday morning. And so, it was only fitting, that she became the first person on earth, ever to see the "RISEN LORD". It is a distinction that she would never have to share with anyone.

What a wonderful earthly reward she had received for her unparalleled love for, and faithfulness to, the SON of the ONLY WISE GOD. And her example of undying faith in GOD is one of the great Sunday school lessons of all times. It is a lesson that every Christian should learn, and then, keep in their hearts to use as fuel, to propel them through their Christian journey here on earth, and into an "Eternal Life" in Heaven with GOD the FATHER, and, CHRIST JESUS, our LORD.

JESUS APPEARS TO THE DISCIPLES
John 20:19-31

20 **(19)** Then the same day at evening, being the first day of the week, when the doors were shut where the disciples were assembled for fear of the Jews, came JESUS and stood in the midst, and saith unto them, "Peace be unto you". **(20)** And when HE had so said, HE shewed unto them HIS hands and HIS side. Then were the disciples glad, when they saw the LORD. **(21)** Then said JESUS to them again, "Peace be unto you: as MY FATHER hath sent ME, even so send I you". **(22)** And when HE had said this, HE breathed on them, and saith unto them, "Receive ye the HOLY GHOST: **(23)** Whose soever sins ye remit, they are remitted unto them; and whose soever sins ye retain, they are retained". **(24)** But Thomas, one of the twelve, called Didymus, was not with them when JESUS came. **(25)** The other disciples therefore said unto him, "We have seen the LORD". But he said unto them, "Except I shall see in HIS hands the print of the nails, and put my finger into the print of the nails, and thrust my hand into HIS side, I will not believe". **(26)** And after eight days again HIS disciples were within, and Thomas with them: then came JESUS, the doors being shut, and stood in the midst, and said, "Peace be unto you". **(27)** Then saith HE to Thomas, "Reach hither thy finger, and behold MY hands; and reach hither thy hand, and thrust it into MY side: and be not faithless, but believing". **(28)** And Thomas answered and said unto HIM, "My LORD and MY GOD". **(29)** JESUS saith unto him, "Thomas, because thou hast seen ME, thou hast believed: blessed are they that have not seen, and yet have believed". **(30)** And many other signs truly did JESUS in the presence of HIS disciples, which are not written in this book: **(31)** But these are written, that ye might believe that

JESUS is the CHRIST, the SON of GOD; and that believing ye might have life through HIS name.

COMMENTARY:

The Christian Church should never endeavor to follow man-made policies, but rather, should always aspire to adhere to the will of CHRIST JESUS. The Church fails when it tries to solve problems within its own wisdom and strength, and omits the will and guidance of GOD, through the Holy Scriptures. When we take matters into our own hands, we show GOD and the world that we doubt the Christian belief structure already put in place by CHRIST, through the holy and divine instructions of GOD the FATHER. It also tends to exhibits that we have an inadequate faith, or, inadequate view of GOD, as far as us trusting in HIS superior wisdom.

In John chapter 20, verses 19-29, JESUS invites all doubters to accept and believe in HIM. We see chronicled in these verses, the first two times JESUS appeared to HIS disciples during the forty-day period following HIS Resurrection. The first occurred on the day of the resurrection, and the second occurred eight days later. On the evening of Resurrection Sunday, the chosen Disciples of CHRIST JESUS were meeting behind locked doors, because they were still afraid of the Jewish leaders. They feared that the Jewish leaders would be seeking to kill them, just as they had slain JESUS, three days earlier. They had not yet received the courage from the HOLY SPIRIT that they would need to carry out the commission charged to them by CHRIST.

Suddenly, JESUS was standing among them saying, "Peace be with you", a phrase HE would repeat three times, twice in the first visit, and once more in the second visit. During these post-Resurrection visits, JESUS was seeking to strengthen and encourage HIS Disciples, and get them to finally believe in HIM. HE sought to instill in them, the "Divine Viewpoint" they would need in order to convince others to also believe. The phrase "HE breathed on them" is translated from the Aramaic idiom meaning, "HE gave them courage". This encouragement came in the form of "the promise of the HOLY SPIRIT".

JESUS tells HIS chosen men in verse 23 that, "If you forgive anyone's sins, they are forgiven, and if you refuse to forgive them, they are unforgiven". This statement has been the subject of much controversial debate over the centuries, and I doubt very seriously if I'm going to clear it up here, but here we go.

The Greek construction is quite literally this "if you forgive anyone his sins, his sins have been forgiven". If you refuse to forgive the sins of others, then, that person's sin will retain you in a spiritual prison. It is in the Gospel, that we proclaim forgiveness, and that forgiveness will set us free from the wrath of unforgiveness that we harbor within ourselves. And so, when we forgive, the sin of unforgiveness is automatically wiped away by the blood of JESUS.

Sharing the Gospel, places us in a role of forgiving, or not forgiving sins, depending on the response of the hearer. When we, as Christians, receive a person's request for salvation, and we subsequently lead them to CHRIST, we are, quite literally, giving that person an opportunity to turn from their sins and turn to GOD, so that their sins can be forgiven. It is the same opportunity that JESUS gives all of us, by way of HIS vicarious sacrifice, and the HOLY SPIRIT in us, bears witness to that (Acts 5:31-32, Ephesians 1:6-8). And while we can only forgive those sins that are directly committed against us personally, it is still the great privilege of the Christian to convey the message of GOD's forgiveness of sin, to mankind.

Eight days later, JESUS re-appears to HIS Disciples. During the first visit, Thomas, who was one of HIS original Disciples, was not present. JESUS, knowing of Thomas' doubts, invites him to examine the wounds scars on HIS hands and in HIS side, so that he too, would finally believe. After Thomas had done this, he proclaimed definitively these words; "my LORD, my GOD! Then JESUS told him "You believe because you have seen ME. Blessed are those who haven't seen ME, and believe anyway". That statement depicts the very fiber of the Christian Faith.

Only those who walk by faith, and believe in CHRIST JESUS, can enter into the Kingdom of Heaven. Thomas never lacked courage, but he was a natural pessimist. There was never any doubt that he loved JESUS, but the cross was only what he humanly expected, just as all the rest did also. They saw death on that cross that Friday, as being the end. And, as a result of JESUS' visits on that Sunday evening, Thomas began to clearly understand that this life was not the final act of the human drama. And so too, should we as Christians, also come to the same realization. JESUS truly is "the Resurrection and the Life, and HE offers that "Eternal Life", to all those who believe in HIM.

WHAT DID WE LEARN FROM CHAPTER TWENTY?
Here are some key points to remember

(1). Mary Magdalene was the first person to arrive at JESUS' tomb on the Sunday of HIS resurrection. (John 20:1)

(2). Peter was the first person to enter into the tomb on Resurrection Sunday. (John 20:5)

(3). JESUS' body was not in the tomb. (John 20:1-10)

(4). JESUS showed HIMSELF first to Mary Magdalene. She was the first person to witness the "Risen" LORD. (John 20:11-18)

(5). On the evening of the first day JESUS appeared to some of HIS disciples, who were behind locked doors. (John 20:19-23)

(6). JESUS gives HIS disciples the power of the HOLY SPIRIT so that they can convey the message of GOD's forgiveness to the world. (John 20:22-23)

(7). Eight days later, JESUS re-appeared to HIS disciples for the benefit of Thomas. (John 20:24-29)

CHAPTER TWENTY-ONE:

(129)

WE ARE CALLED TO BE FISHERS OF MEN: OBEY THE LORD

SCRIPTURE:
The King James Version
John 21:1-8

21 **(1)** After these things JESUS shewed HIMSELF again to the disciples at the sea of Tiberias; and on this wise shewed HE HIMSELF. **(2)** There were together Simon Peter, and Thomas called Didymus, and Nathanael of Cana in Galilee, and the sons of Zebedee, and two other of HIS disciples. **(3)** Simon Peter saith unto them, "I go a fishing". They say unto him, "We also go with thee". They went forth, and entered into a ship immediately; and that night they caught nothing. **(4)** But when the morning was now com, JESUS stood on the shore: but the disciples knew not that it was JESUS. **(5)** Then JESUS saith unto them, "Children, have ye any meat?" They answered HIM, "No". **(6)** And HE said unto them, "Cast the net on the right side of the ship, and ye shall find". They cast therefore, and now they were not able to draw it for the multitude of fishes. **(7)** Therefore that disciple whom JESUS loved saith unto Peter, "It is the LORD". Now when Simon Peter heard that it was the LORD, he girt his fisher's coat unto him, (for he was naked,) and did cast himself into the sea. **(8)** And the other disciples came in a little ship; (for they were not far from land, but as it were two hundred cupits,) dragging the net with fishes.

COMMENTARY:

In the epilogue to this gospel account of the Apostle John, he seeks to show us how JESUS re-instated Peter, following his latest bout with failure, namely, his blatant denial of even knowing our LORD and SAVIOR, during HIS "passion" hours in Jerusalem. JESUS had already promised to meet with HIS disciples in Galilee (Matthew 28:7), and so, here we are in a scene at the Sea of Galilee, otherwise known as the Sea of Tiberias.

Here in John 21, we find that Peter had led many of the disciples back into the trade from which JESUS had called them some three years earlier. However, their lack of success in their old profession stands as evidence as to why we should not try and return to a place where the LORD has already removed us from, so that HE can better use us for HIS purpose. JESUS tells us too, that, apart from HIM, we can do nothing anyway.

When JESUS calls us, not only does that often call for a change of occupation, it also always calls for us to change our ways, and our thinking completely, and, we will no longer feel any real satisfaction in the old lifestyle. Peter must have, no doubt, been feeling pretty low about his denial of CHRIST JESUS, and was desperately seeking to find acceptance back in his old fishing career. We should never allow our sin to drive us away from the LORD, but rather, one should let their sins stand as proof that we cannot live life correctly apart from the LORD.

After Peter and the other disciples had been out all night fishing without catching a single fish, JESUS instructs them to cast their nets on the "right side" of the boat (v.6), where they would catch many fish. The disciples were obedient and did as the LORD said, and as a result, they were overwhelmed with success.

This incident prompted the men to recognize that the LORD was still with them. HE had given them a commission to obey and their old style of fishing was not going to work for them anymore. They were to now lay down their old nets that were used to catch fish for physical food, and pick up their new "spiritual nets", and become fishers of men.

JESUS had shown them during HIS three-year ministry, how to fish from the "right side" of the boat, and now, it was time for them to implement those teachings, and the whole world would serve as their new fishing waters, where their harvest would be exceedingly great.

WE ARE CALLED TO BE SHEPHERDS: LOVE THE LORD
John 21:9-18

21 **(9)** As soon then as they were come to land, they saw a fire of coals there, and fish laid thereon, and bread. **(10)** JESUS saith unto them, "Bring of the fish which ye have now caught". **(11)** Simon Peter went up, and drew the net to land full of great fishes, an hundred and fifty and three: and for all there were so many, yet was not the net broken. **(12)** JESUS saith unto them, "Come and dine". And none of the disciples durst ask HIM, "WHO art THOU? Knowing that it was the LORD. **(13)** JESUS then cometh, and taketh bread, and giveth them, and fish likewise. **(14)** This is now the third time that JESUS shewed HIMSELF to HIS disciples, after that HE was risen from the dead. **(15)** So when they had dined, JESUS saith to Simon Peter, "Simon, son of Jonas, lovest thou ME more than these? He saith unto HIM, "Yea, LORD; THOU knowest that I love THEE". He saith unto him, "Feed MY lambs". **(16)** HE saith to him again the second time, "Simon, son of Jonas, lovest thou ME?" He saith unto HIM, "Yea, LORD; THOU knowest that I love THEE. HE saith unto him, "Feed MY sheep". (17) HE saith unto him the third time, "Simon, son of Jonas, lovest thou ME?" Peter grieved because HE said unto him the third time, "Lovest thou ME?" and he said unto HIM, "LORD. THOU knowest all things; THOU knowest that I love THEE". JESUS saith unto him, "Feed MY sheep". (18) "Verily, verily, I say unto thee, "When thou wast young, thou girdedst thyself, and walkedst whither thou wouldest: but when thou shalt be old, thou shalt stretch forth thy hands, and another shall gird thee, and carry thee whither thou wouldest not."

COMMENTARY:

In John 18:27, Peter denied JESUS for the third and final time. It was H.G. Welles who said, "A man can be a bad musician, and yet, be passionately in love with music". And so, for whatever Peter did, and no matter how terrible his failure was, there was never truly any doubt that he was passionately devoted to JESUS. He may have been overconfident at times, as he was when he told JESUS that he would never deny HIM. However, sometimes when a man says, "That's the one thing I will never do", then, that's the very thing that he needs to carefully guard against doing.

Satan often attacks a person at a point where they are most sure of themselves, because he knows that it is there, where they are most likely to be unprepared. The shame of failure and disloyalty is not altogether a lost, because it often gives us a feeling of sympathy and understanding, that, otherwise, we may have never had.

"Do you love ME?" is what JESUS asked Peter, three times, here in John 21, and I guess, the only way that we can prove our love for JESUS is by loving others. Love is the greatest privilege in the world, yet, it brings with it, the greatest responsibility, and for Peter, it brought, a cross, and he did die for the LORD, because he too eventually died on a cross, and as Jewish tradition has it, he requested to be nailed upside down, because he felt unworthy to die in the same manner as CHRIST.

Love always involves responsibility, and it always involves a sacrifice. We don't really love JESUS, unless we are willing to take on HIS task, and, to take up our own cross. We may never be able to write, or think, like the Apostle John, and in fact, we may never even be able to travel to the ends of the earth and preach like Paul. But here's where we can all follow in the footsteps of Peter. If we love JESUS, each of us can help someone else guard against going astray. And if we love JESUS, each of us can love one another. And finally, if we love JESUS, each of us has an open opportunity to feed JESUS' sheep, with the loving and nourishing food, of the "Word of GOD".

WE ARE CALLED TO BE DISCIPLES: FOLLOW THE LORD
John 21:19-25

21 19) This spake HE, signifying by what death he should glorify GOD. And when HE had spoken this, HE saith unto him, "Follow ME". **(20)** Then Peter, turning about, seeth the disciple whom JESUS loved following; which also leaned on HIS breast at supper, and said, "LORD, which is he that betrayeth THEE?" **(21)** Peter seeing him saith to JESUS, "LORD, and what shall this man do?" **(22)** JESUS saith unto him, "If I will that he tarry till I come, what is that to thee? Follow thou ME. **(23)** Then went this saying abroad among the brethren, that that disciple should not die: yet JESUS said not unto him, "He shall not die;" but, "If I will that he tarry till I come, what is that to thee?" **(24)** This is the disciple which testifieth of these things, and wrote these things: and we know that his testimony is true. **(25)** And there are also many other things which JESUS did, the which, if they should be written every one, I suppose that even the world itself could not contain the books that should be written. Amen.

COMMENTARY:

Obedience to JESUS' command to "Follow ME" is the key issue in every Christian life. We must follow the LORD's path wherever it leads us personally, whether it leads to a cross, or, to some other difficult undertaking in life. The important thing is that we concentrate on following where JESUS leads us as individuals. And at the same time, we must be careful that we don't interfere with where GOD is leading other Christians in the Church.

Remember, the church is not a hierarchy like the one that was established by the Sanhedrin in New Testament biblical times. It is not a place where the overseers can tell others what GOD's plan is for them. The church is an organism of living believers who are directly connected to JESUS CHRIST, the LIVING HEAD of the Church, and each member is responsible to love and follow HIM in the form of a personal experiential relationship.

After being informed by JESUS how he would personally glorify GOD in death, Peter immediately became curious as to what fate the apostle John would encounter. Here we see JESUS sharply rebukes HIS newly reinstated lead disciple, as HE, in effect, tells him to only be concerned with his own personal calling, and to not concern himself with the callings of others.

GOD has a personal plan for each of us, and the only way we can successfully do GOD's will, is by staying focused on our own calling or task. In order to fulfill the role of a disciple, we must be willing to take up our own cross and follow JESUS where HE leads us, personally. We can't afford to become distracted by someone else's ministry, or become envious of what GOD is doing in someone else's life, just because it may seem to be more glamorous than our own task. GOD chooses us for ministries that HE has already equipped us to do, personally, and HE expects us to be obedient in carrying out that mission, HIS way, not ours. HIS plans for us will always vary, and HIS reasons are seldom revealed to anyone.

The apostle John witnessed all of the events written about in his book, and he wrote all of these things under the influence and power of the HOLY SPIRIT. His book ends showing us a picture of himself and Peter following our LORD and SAVIOR into the unknown. They were walking out and following JESUS on faith, right into the pages of the Book of Acts. They now had their own personal special assignments, and they were ready to carry them out together, yet in different ways, to each, his own.

And this now obscure, little sect of followers called "Adherents of the Way" was about to explode into the first century and quickly become the most important offering the world has ever known. They would become known, the world over, as "Christians", and their organization would carry, as its greatest perk, "the gift of Salvation".

WHAT DID WE LEARN FROM CHAPTER TWENTY-ONE?
Here are some key points to remember

(1). Christians are called to be Fishers of Men. We are not to return to our old way of life, as JESUS will then show us how to fish from the right side of the boat and be successful at it. (John 21:1-8)

(2). Christians are called to be shepherds, and to love the LORD our GOD. (John 21:9-18)

(3). Christians are called to be disciples, and to follow JESUS. (John 21:19-23)

(4). In John 18, Peter publicly denied JESUS three times. Here in John 21, he is Reinstated by JESUS publicly, with the trice repeated question of, "Do you love ME? (John 21:15-17)

(5). JESUS revealed to Peter what kind of death he would die to glorify GOD. (John 21:18-19)

(6). Every Christian must stay focused on their own calling, and not be so concerned about GOD's calling on another person's life. (John 21:20-23

(7). The appearance of JESUS to HIS disciples on the banks of the Sea of Galilee was the third appearance to them, following HIS resurrection. (John 21:14)

CLOSING REMARKS

IT is a life-changing thing, getting to know, and becoming accustomed to practicing the word of GOD. GOD's word has already come, in fact, it has been with us since the beginning, and it simply cannot be, nor, will not be disregarded. The word of GOD is synonymous with life, and therefore, HIS word is effective and penetrating, and, it absolutely scrutinizes all of our thoughts, desires, and intentions.

All things lay naked before GOD. HE sees all, hears all, and knows all that we do. And every one of us will have to make an account for the deeds done in our lifetimes. And, whether or not we believe that HE exists, therefore, becomes totally irrelevant.

And now, all glory be to YOU GOD, WHO is able to keep us from falling, over and over again, and then finally, bring us into YOUR OWN glorious presence, absolutely innocent of sin, and then YOU do it with exceeding, unspeakable joy. That's why YOU are truly the ONLY WISE GOD, and, our SAVIOR, through JESUS CHRIST, and unto YOU be glory and majesty, dominion and power, in the beginning, now, and through all the ages of eternity. THY will be done. Amen.

www.ingramcontent.com/pod-product-compliance
Lightning Source LLC
Chambersburg PA
CBHW081231090426
42738CB00016B/3255